D0921237

A Man
Born Again

*Other titles by John E. Beahn
in the TAN Legends Series*

A MAN CLEANSED BY GOD
A Novel Based on the Life of Saint Patrick

A MAN OF GOOD ZEAL
A Novel Based on the Life of Saint Frances de Sales

A RICH YOUNG MAN
A Novel Based on the Life of Saint Anthony of Padua

A Man Born Again

Born Again

A Novel Based on the
Life of Saint Thomas More

JOHN E. BEAHN

TAN Books
Charlotte, North Carolina

This book was first published in 1954 by Bruce Publishing Company, Milwaukee, Wisconsin, under the title *A Man Born Again: St. Thomas More*. This TAN Legends edition has been re-typeset and revised to include corrections of typographical errors and updating of punctuation, spelling, and diction.

TAN Legends edition copyright © 2013 TAN Books.

Cover design by Caroline Kiser.

Cover Image: *Sir Thomas More* (engraving, 1477–1535) by Holbein the Younger, Hans (1497/8–1543) (after). Private Collection, Ken Welsh. The Bridgeman Art Library.

ISBN: 978-0-9675978-5-0

Cataloging-in-Publication data on file with the Library of Congress.

Printed and bound in the United States of America.

TAN Books
Charlotte, North Carolina
www.TANBooks.com
2013

To My Parents,
Brothers, and Sisters

And there was a man of the Pharisees, named Nicodemus, a ruler of the Jews. This man came to Jesus by night, and said to him: Rabbi, we know that thou art come a teacher from God; for no man can do these signs which thou dost, unless God be with him.

Jesus answered, and said to him: Amen, amen I say to thee, unless a man be born again, he cannot see the kingdom of God.

Nicodemus saith to him: How can a man be born when he is old? can he enter a second time into his mother's womb, and be born again?

Jesus answered: Amen, amen I say to thee, unless a man be born again of water and the Holy Ghost, he cannot enter into the kingdom of God. That which is born of the flesh, is flesh; and that which is born of the Spirit, is spirit. Wonder not, that I said to thee, you must be born again. The Spirit breatheth where he will; and thou hearest his voice, but thou knowest not whence he cometh, and whither he goeth: so is everyone who is born of the Spirit.

John 3:1–8

BOOK I

1

"THOMAS More, Londoner-born . . ."—thus I began two years ago the epitaph for the tomb in which I thought I should someday lie. At that time, I encouraged myself to believe that I should die quietly and peacefully, surrounded by my family, comforted as to their material welfare when I was no longer with them, strengthened by their prayers and the prayers of priests at my bedside. Had I thought beyond the actual moment of death, I would have imagined my funeral cortege, moving from the parish church through the streets of Chelsea, followed by some number of my friends, to the tomb in the chapel of my own great house.

I know now—I have known since this morning—that my body will never rest in such a peaceful place. I know that my body will be tumbled from the executioner's platform into an unmarked grave on Tower Hill; I know that my head will stand sentry atop a pike on London Bridge to appease the King's anger.

No man has informed me of this; neither King nor Council have yet decreed my death. I know not the exact manner in which I was informed. I know only that I was informed, fully and completely, this morning when I wrote to Father Leder assuring him that I had not and would not subscribe the oath demanded by the King. "I know," I wrote, "that if ever I should swear it, I should swear against my conscience; and I am very sure in my mind that I shall never be able to change my conscience to the contrary."

I stopped my writing at that point, astonished by the confidence of my assertion that I would not change my conscience. Ever before, when a statement was required of me, I offered my willingness to be instructed by others and to change my conscience if someone show me wherein it be wrong. A humble and prudent man does not cling stubbornly to the dictate of his own conscience when other good and spiritual men follow a different way. Rather does he strive to turn his conscience by study and meditation, by mortification and prayer. All these I did; I felt that I had not been a man of such holy life that I could boldly offer myself to death. Rather than protest the cause of my conscience, I had drawn back lest God, for my presumption, suffer me to fall away from Him. Now I am confirmed and resolutely determined to follow the direction pointed by my conscience even though the end be death. God Himself leads me to it, and I trust in His great mercy that He will give me grace to endure.

Illusion?

"God speaks to a man," wrote St. Augustine from his own great experience and knowledge, "not by dinning in his ears nor even by means of angels, but by evident truth manifest to him who is prepared to hear with the mind rather than the body. For He speaks to that faculty of man which is greater than all else in him, and which is excelled only by God Himself."

In such manner was I informed. The knowledge of the manner of my death is but one facet of a sublime knowledge by which I foresee my death from without and perceive also the mystery of the hand of God working secretly within. Not this January morning of the year 1535 did God first become my Guide to lead me only to my death. As far back as memory reveals the past, I discern His hand, now leading, now urging, now turning, now drawing me back, as ever He will to each of us in this mortal life if we flee not away from Him and the path He bids each to follow.

I claim not to understand this mystery of His mercy nor by what means He accomplishes it in others. I can analyze only my own life and, perhaps, but little and obscurely understand His great grace in me. Yet each remembered incident and each remembered circumstance and each remembered friend (and enemy) arouses new wonder, new gratitude, new joy to such extent that I desire no longer to write; I desire only to multiply my memories that I may multiply my thanks to Him who has so lavished His grace in me.

My present situation, uncomfortable as confined, encourages my purpose. The King has again forbidden visitors, and my thoughts shall be interrupted only by the attendants or, possibly, by members of the Council returning to interrogate me. The table, the stone walls and floor of my cell, the wooden door, the straw mat of my bed, and the bench on which I sit offer little possibility of distraction. If a man prayed God for the opportunity of contemplating Him and His mercy, his prayer could not be better answered.

From the window of my cell, I can look down on London to refresh memory by sight of the places where occurred many of the incidents of my life. Roofs and chimney pots of the houses are well below the level where I am confined. Almost at a glance, I can see the entire area of the city, as far as the west wall or even beyond, and from the Thames at my left to the north wall at the extreme right. I can see but little into the streets; they are hidden from me by our custom of building houses with the upper stories projecting over the streets, shutting them off from the sun by day and making them dark, forbidding tunnels by night.

I need no sight of the streets. The Londoner-born can see well the crowds that fill the streets from first morning light, can see their misery and the greater misery to come. The Londoner-born can hear their voices that once lifted to glorify God but now lift only to hail a king who thinks to make himself a god. Because they are my people, I can see them in my heart as readily as in my mind.

Below me, the line formed by rooftops and chimney pots guides my eyes along the direction of the streets which begin at the base of this tower prison and wind their way irregularly away from me. At intervals, their path is broken by other streets which begin at the Thames, on my left, and pass northward through the city to the wall. In the middle distance, straight before me, I can see the towers of St. Paul's.

St. Paul's is the center of the scene of my early life. A short distance before it, not discernible to the eyes but manifest to memory, is the house on Milk Street where I was born and where I lived with my father, my stepmother, my brothers and sisters during the first twelve years of my life. My mother died when I was so young that I have no memory of her.

Somewhat nearer and to the right, a sweeping curve of rooftops marks the beginning of Threadneedle Street. There would be St. Anthony's, where I attended school until I was twelve and first acquired knowledge of Latin and English, of rhetoric and mathematics.

Schooling and home life ended on my twelfth birthday. On that day in February of 1490, my father conducted me across the bridge and along the other bank of the river to Lambeth Palace, residence of Archbishop Morton, Lord Chancellor of England. There I was entered as a page in the service of His Grace to learn discipline from his secretaries and manners from his guests. Had I been attentive toward His Grace and the chaplains, and learned humility of them, God might have directed my life in other channels; but I was attentive rather to manners and learning, mindful of the things esteemed by the world, not yet alert to the things esteemed by God.

2

FROM the beginning, I was sufficiently liked by the other pages and accepted by them; yet was I also resented because of my education. Being smallest of them, I could not compete against them physically, but I realized shortly, and made them also realize, that I was superior in wit and quickness of tongue. Thus, my relations alternated from day to day, being in good favor one day and disfavor the next.

For some cause now forgotten, I was excluded from a Christmas play my companions planned for entertainment of His Grace and his guests. The exclusion offended me, and I resorted to what I thought was my superior wit to avenge the slight, planning how I might disrupt their play.

On the night of the play—the night after my first Christmas at Lambeth—His Grace's study was warm with the heat from the great fireplace, the banks of candles, and from the press of all those present to see the play. Manuscript racks had been removed for this one night and a raised platform placed across the end of the room before the great windows. Archbishop Morton had himself directed placement of his chair some six feet in front of the platform, with long benches on either side for his guests. Behind were members of the household.

While the play progressed, I edged forward carefully

along the side of the room until I gained a place at the very corner of the platform. I had not to wait long for an opportunity. Three of my fellow pages, costumed as shepherds, appeared from behind a drapery and moved timidly forward.

"This has been a wondrous night, my brothers," said one so softly that the words could not have been heard beyond the edge of the platform.

"Let us go over to Bethlehem and see this word that has come to pass, my brothers," a second shepherd whispered.

I leaped to the stage and confronted the three. "Turn back!" I shouted. "Turn back! Wolves are among the sheep, my brothers." My shout, contrasting with the inaudible whisperings of the shepherds, startled those in the room as it frightened the three before me. I was aware that the Archbishop suddenly jerked his head upward as though, perhaps, he had been sleeping, and I heard a stir among the others in the room. "Turn back!" I shouted once more.

The three did indeed turn back, pushing each other and stumbling in their haste to escape. The last one fell just before gaining refuge behind the drapery. I had already jumped down from the platform when I heard a guest on the bench laugh loudly at the frantic efforts of the three; the rest of the room quickly joined him. I dodged through the crowd and escaped.

I did not go to the pages' quarters that night, mindful of my small size and the anger of the others. I made my bed in an unoccupied room, well satisfied with my efforts of the evening.

In the morning, immediately after Mass, my self-satisfaction was destroyed by a summons to appear before His Grace. Until then, I had not thought that His Grace would concern himself with the retribution I had visited on the others. When I stood before His Grace's desk and felt his disapproval, I trembled.

He was a wide-shouldered man, and the tall-backed chair made his shoulders seem even wider. When he was young, he had been a very powerful man; now when age had sapped his physical strength, office conferred on him a dignity even more impressive. I was a small boy and a miscreant standing before him who was holder of the highest office of the Church in England and also Lord Chancellor to the King.

"Explain, boy! Explain!" he prompted me impatiently.

Desperately but more timidly than the shepherds in the night's play, I stumbled and faltered. "The others resent me that I am educated," I pleaded.

The great man moved some papers about on his desk until he uncovered a small book. He turned the pages rapidly until he found what he sought, then thrust the book toward me. "If you are well educated, boy, translate this for me."

I glanced at the Latin and saw that it was not difficult. "All men," I translated, "desire knowledge; but of what value is knowledge without fear of the Lord? The lowly and ignorant who serve God are wiser than proud philosophers who neglect their souls while they contemplate the course of the stars. A man who knows himself well esteems himself but little and does not glory in the praises of men. If I should know all mysteries and all knowledge but have not charity, what will it avail me before the judgment seat of God?

"Do not be vain of your talents or knowledge; rather dread the fame these bring. If you seem to know much, recognize that much you do not know; remember your ignorance rather than your knowledge. Why strive to exalt yourself when so many others are better educated or more learned? If you would be truly learned, learn to love obscurity. The most beneficial learning is a true knowledge of self, recognition of fault, humility as to self and charity as to others—in this is the greatest wisdom. . . ."

"That is sufficient, young More," His Grace interrupted. I sensed, with that perceptiveness of boyhood, that his manner toward me had softened. "Tell me of your education," he said.

I told him of St. Anthony's, of Master Holt, my teacher, and of my love for reading. I was glad he had turned from the subject of my transgression.

"God has given you tremendous talents, boy," His Grace told me. He shook his head slowly and disapprovingly. "He did not give those gifts that you might humiliate others. He gave them to you to use for His purposes. When He gives such gifts, He often allows temptations to come against those very gifts."

Thus did God draw good from evil, causing His Grace to notice me and learn of my gifts. From that ordeal, I emerged with some favor and with His Grace's permission to improve my reading and language by making use of his own manuscripts. Often he questioned me about a manuscript I had read. Boylike, I forgot the lesson he had made me read and his advice to me.

3

B Y the natural progression of older pages to other positions in the palace and by departure of some, I became, late in November of 1491, senior page, a position requiring me to sit quietly on a bench inside His Grace's study, ready to do whatever errand His Grace might wish.

Through the first three weeks of that month, a thick fog lay close to the earth. Only rarely and for short minutes during those weeks did it lift sufficiently to see the King's palace at Westminster across the river from Lambeth. During that time, no guests arrived at Lambeth nor messengers from the King. Communications ceased between the King at Westminster on the one side of the river and the Archbishop-Lord Chancellor at Lambeth on the other.

I was disappointed in the first hours of my new position that I had no more to do than sit very still on my bench while His Grace attended to papers on his desk without once sending me on an errand. I had expected to be sent on numberless trips to his first secretary or to his comptroller or to the treasurer or to some of the gentlemen of the household. Instead, I sat for a seemingly endless time while my attention shifted from the aged figure of His Grace to the racks of manuscripts along the sides of the room, or to the great windows which permitted only a view of the fog.

"Master More!"

An errand at last. I slipped from the bench, approached His Grace as quickly as discipline permitted, and stood before his desk.

"Were you sleeping, Master More?"

The unexpected question startled and dismayed me. "No, Your Grace," I protested uncertainly. His expression was very stern.

He smiled as unexpectedly as he had frightened me. He let his broad body relax against the back of his chair, then took the square cap from his head and put it on his desk—something he did only when he was amused. I felt relieved and smiled also.

"Your service will soon end, Master More?"

"My birthday is February 7, Your Grace."

"And then, young More? What then will you become?"

I had not thought of what I should become after my service to the Archbishop ended.

"Will you be a scribe or an usher or a third secretary?" His Grace prompted. "You will never be sufficiently large to be a member of the guard."

"My father said I am to be a lawyer, Your Grace," I answered at last.

His Grace restored the square cap to his head as though no longer amused. "Lawyer!" he repeated. "Did you learn Latin and English and did I permit you to read manuscripts here"—he motioned toward the racks behind me—"that you would become a lawyer?"

I stood uncomfortably before him without courage to answer his indignant question. I could not repeat that it was my father's wish, and I would not admit that it was not my wish.

His Grace's manner softened again so that he was, at

the same moment, a kindly gray-haired patron, the dignified Archbishop, and the powerful Lord Chancellor of all England. "What do you wish for yourself, boy?" he inquired.

A dream returned to my mind, a dream that had many times recurred to me but which never could propose itself seriously. "I should like to be a writer of great books, Your Grace."

I could see that the answer surprised him, yet pleased him also. For a moment, I thought he would laugh at my words as older people often do at the dreams of the young and as my father had, but I watched and saw that his smile revealed no amusement, only pleasure and approval.

"You will need more learning, boy," he said.

I nodded my head, forgetful of manners and discipline alike, for his comment made me unhappily aware that my days of reading his manuscripts were soon to end. No one referred to law as a form of learning; all referred to it as a "reading" of the law.

"You should study at Oxford, Master More," His Grace continued.

A wild hope surged through me, and the dream that lay half-hidden within me became a goal possible of achievement. His Grace did not promise, nor did his tone of voice indicate more than calm observation; but a thirteen-year-old boy, possessed of a dream, needs little encouragement to grant freedom to imagination.

From that day, I was a model of decorum and of diligence in the performance of duty. Each errand was an occasion to demonstrate swiftness of movement; each command was an invitation to display willingness of effort. I knew that I pleased His Grace even though he said nothing more to me of writing nor of Oxford.

As the days of January passed and my fourteenth birthday drew near, I wavered between relief that my term of service would soon end and fear that His Grace had forgotten completely his suggestion about my studying at Oxford. I did not abandon hope, but I contemplated more frequently the disagreeable prospect of returning to my father's house on Milk Street and being entered into law school. I even suffered the fear that the eagerness of my efforts had, in some manner, persuaded His Grace to believe that I should be a servant to some noble rather than a writer of great books and that his letter of commendation would be designed toward that end rather than to the fulfillment of my dream.

My father arrived very early on the morning of my fourteenth birthday, certain indication that he expected pleasure from the visit. When I was summoned to the Great Entrance, he was already entertaining the guards and being entertained by them. The friendliness of the guards toward him was unusual, for those tall and muscular men seldom looked favorably on soft, pudgy men as small as my father. When I entered the guards' room, he was sitting pompously erect on a bench, delighting the guards by describing with what dignity he would converse with the Archbishop-Lord Chancellor. When he had greeted me, he placed one arm over my shoulders, and we stood facing the group of guards. "My boy will receive the finest letter of commendation His Grace ever wrote," he declaimed. His boast seemed a signal for the group to disperse.

So enraptured was my father by the privilege of entering Lambeth, this one day, through the entrance used by ambassadors and guests that he did not notice my silence. When a page came to summon us, my father delayed for a moment to whisper earnestly to me, "The Chancellor will receive us today as he does those great men, the ambassadors. Keep that thought in mind, son, and conduct yourself accordingly in the presence of His Grace."

Oppressed with my forebodings and little interested in the reception by His Grace, I remembered my father's words about ambassadors only because he displayed neither poise nor assurance in the presence of the Archbishop. Whenever my father spoke, he bowed forward and, when the Archbishop spoke, my father again bowed forward, conduct I knew to be wrong because even the pages were trained to stand erect when addressing His Grace and to bow only when leaving his presence.

I had greater difficulty standing erect that morning than at any other time of my service, for His Grace enumerated both my virtues and vices, but he elaborated my vices while hurrying quickly past my virtues.

"Mister More," he concluded, "your son has talents which can destroy him if his pride is not curbed; but talents which can take him far—toward heaven, we hope—if they are joined with humility. That both his learning and his humility may be developed together, I have arranged for your son to enter Canterbury Hall at Oxford."

My heart leaped at his announcement, for all that His Grace had said indicated that he had forgotten completely our conversation more than two months earlier.

"That will not be necessary," I heard my father answer, and the surge of exultation in me quieted. "The boy will be a lawyer. He can enter New Inn immediately and begin reading of the law."

I held my eyes hopefully on Archbishop Morton and was encouraged by his small frown.

"Lawyer?" he demanded. He spoke the word almost contemptuously. "Would you waste . . . ?" he began, then glanced toward me. "Anyone who can read can become a lawyer, Mister More. Permit the boy to develop his talents and character before you commit him to that life."

The smile had disappeared from my father's round face, and he was troubled. "To send him to Oxford would be to start him toward the priesthood, Your Grace."

Archbishop Morton's frown increased. "And do you suffer 'lawyers' envy,' Mister More, as so many of your profession?"

I felt that I was hunching my shoulders anxiously. I had heard that term when chaplains talked of those lawyers who envied the positions held by the clergy. I knew His Grace referred to those lawyers who coveted service with the King, hoping to become wealthy. I could not think of my father as envying anyone, especially the priests in the service of the King.

"I envy neither priest nor bishop who serves the King, Your Grace," my father said firmly. "I know I could not serve him as well."

I was relieved as I saw the Archbishop relax. "I commend your humility, Mister More," he said.

My father persisted. "But my boy has not a priestly vocation, Your Grace," he said.

"If Oxford prepares some to be priests, it prepares more to be scholars."

My father shook his head slowly and doubtfully as though to disagree without disrespect. "Your Grace, I am not so rich that my boy can become a scholar. He would do well to imitate his betters without striving to equal them."

The answer amused His Grace. "Now, Mister More, you are confusing humility with pusillanimity," he said, laughing.

My father smiled, but I knew that he did not understand the word His Grace had used and could not answer for fear of offending. As though accepting my father's silence for agreement, His Grace handed him the letter about my service and dismissed us. Then, strangely, it was I who remembered to bow to the Archbishop while my father forgot completely his admonitions to me as to our conduct, turned away abruptly, and walked from the room without bowing.

4

HIS manner toward me as we walked into London and during the week required for preparation was reserved and resentful as though he considered me responsible for the action of the Archbishop. I was most careful that my conduct would not increase his objections and restrained my tongue from comments that might prolong them.

I was well able to be generous for I had the beginning of that future I desired and, I soon discovered, I had also achieved tremendous stature in the eyes of others. I was known as a protégé of His Grace, Archbishop Morton, Lord Chancellor of England. Along Milk Street, men and women called out their greetings. My sister, Joan, almost seventeen and preparing for her marriage, took me to visit the family of her affianced and presented me triumphantly and proudly as her brother—a most unique event in the life of any younger brother. At St. Paul's after Mass, my father's friends and acquaintances of the law courts congratulated me and wished me well for the future. The good wishes and congratulations of these lawyers, envious of the priests as they were, made me realize that His Grace's favor had made me a celebrity. Seekers of worldly success themselves, they valued what had been conferred on me.

At Oxford, the power of Archbishop Morton's name was again demonstrated. On the morning following my arrival, I had put my clothing and my few most treasured possessions into the chest my roommates had designated as mine and stood, for a time, at the window overlooking the court. Students and masters, moving from their lodgings to lecture rooms, crowded the area below me. My new roommates had told me, during the brief interval between Mass and their departure, that I must first visit the registrar. I was considering uncertainly whether to seek that official immediately or wait until one of my roommates would be free to serve as guide.

"Master More?"

I swung around to the doorway, smiling my response to that pleasant voice even before I saw its owner. In the doorway, his appearance as pleasant as his voice, was a tall young priest, handsome despite his large nose. The friendliness of his smile overwhelmed whatever might have detracted from his appearance.

"I am Father Colet," he announced. His smile widened. "His Grace, Archbishop Morton, wrote that I should call immediately on Master Thomas More for the improvement of my Latin and English."

My spirits soared, and I laughed self-consciously as I shook hands with him. "My father knows your father," I said before I realized that perhaps everyone in London knew Sir Henry Colet but that Sir Henry did not know all in London.

"Then we are family friends, More," he answered, as though completely delighted with the discovery and unaware of social disparity between us. He had come, he told me, to conduct me to the registrar and then to guide me about the university. I tried to invent excuses for him to leave me because I was made uncomfortable by having for my guide a man who was both priest and the son of Sir Henry, but he laughed at my protests and said: "If I should not serve as guide to Thomas More, I must still serve as guide to a protégé of the Archbishop."

After dinner that same day, Father Colet returned again with the news that we were invited to visit Master Grocyn. My expression must have disclosed bewilderment at the name and at Father Colet's obvious pleasure. "Master Grocyn is England's greatest master of Latin, Greek, and all learning, More. I am inclined to think he is the greatest mind in England."

Master Grocyn was much older than Father Colet. The hair bulging from below his master's cap was more gray than black. His appearance, however, was not at all what I expected it to be, for he had a coarse skin and a bulky body, rather than the pallid slenderness I associated with scholarship. His manner was also strange, for he conducted himself almost with haughtiness. He welcomed us pleasantly but condescendingly; and he astonished me particularly by his patronizing manner toward Father Colet, whom he called "Colet" as casually as the priest addressed me as "More." He seemed ever conscious that he was, as Father Colet had described him, "the greatest mind in England."

There was warmth and graciousness in his manner when Father Colet presented me and told that my patron was Archbishop Morton. "I am impressed, More," he said evenly and seriously. "If you needed a patron, His Grace would not be patron to you; since he is your patron, I know you need none." I felt that, for the first time in my life, I had been addressed as an individual and no longer as a child.

The Master's room was pleasant with two windows side by side. Against one of these was a desk with a chair half-turned from it. His bed in a corner, a chest of drawers, and four chairs still allowed what seemed an excessive amount of space. His fireplace was not large, but the room was comfortably warm. From my own chair, where I was allowed to sit undisturbed while master and priest talked, I looked about for manuscripts or other indications of learning, but I saw none. Perhaps Master Grocyn's learning was so great he no longer had need for such implements. On the desk at the window was a great heap of letters, some of which seemed quite long.

Master Grocyn lectured Father Colet at length about the continent of Europe in general and Italy in particular, pausing frequently to permit the priest to write names of individuals and their locations. After a time, Father Colet seemed to notice my isolation and recited to the Master my accomplishments in Latin and English, which he could have learned only from Archbishop Morton. Master Grocyn then turned his attention to me, questioning me to such extent that I finally realized he was subjecting me to an informal examination.

Several times during this examination, Father Colet smiled and nodded encouragement. Then, when the visit ended and we had walked a short distance from the Master's lodgings, Father Colet suddenly clapped his hands together. "You did excellently, More."

I smiled because he was so pleased but without understanding the cause of his pleasure.

"Tomorrow," he said, "or not later than the day following, the registrar will tell you that Master Grocyn has accepted you in his lecture class."

His explanation did not clarify matters completely for me, but I enjoyed the feeling that the visit with Master

Grocyn had gained for me the esteem of this young and friendly priest. The feeling brought with it an uncomfortable self-consciousness, and I sought some means of diverting attention from myself. "Master Grocyn has traveled all over the world," I observed.

Father Colet laughed. "Not quite all. He studied in Europe, mainly in Italy. He was lecturing me so that I would visit the best schools and seek the best masters when I am there."

I felt an intense dismay. "Are you going to Italy?"

"I shall leave early next week."

The pleasure of that day ended abruptly. Within a matter of hours, I had been lifted from my initial status of new student and stranger at Oxford to the dignity of friendship with Father Colet and admission to the lectures of Master Grocyn. Within a matter of seconds, I had been tumbled downward by news of Father Colet's impending departure.

The hall was quiet when we returned. "My roommates are still in the lecture rooms, I suppose." I hoped that Father Colet would invite me to continue further with him instead of dismissing me to return to the empty room.

"Either in the lecture rooms or in town," Father Colet answered. His expression changed while he spoke, as though his remark reminded him of something serious. "More, you will find that some of those in your hall prefer to spend more of their time in the town than in the lecture rooms. Instead of learning, they study more earnestly how to amuse themselves." He smiled slightly as though apologizing. "I will not give you a sermon so soon after your arrival at Oxford; but you must resolve to be worthy of Master Grocyn's lectures and of His Grace's confidence in you."

I moved my head dolefully. "I have no money to spend in the town," I assured him. "I must report to my father whatever I spend, and he cannot send money to be spent for pleasure."

During the five days preceding the departure of Father Colet, my dejection retreated gradually as I found companionship with my roommates and others in the hall, and immediate encouragement in Master Grocyn's lecture room. I was able to enjoy the brief period of friendship with the priest and to accept the fact of his departure more easily than his first announcement of it.

5

STUDY emerged as the best antidote for my loss of Father Colet. I could not join the other students on their forays into town, a circumstance that separated me from them. For lack of other devices, I went most often to the library to gorge myself with reading, not then realizing that I was enlarging my studies and that the matter I absorbed was made evident to the masters by my answers in the lecture rooms.

In May, Master Grocyn called me to his room and put me to work translating a Latin manuscript. He had installed another table at the second window for my use, and I worked diligently, aware that the term would soon end and I had barely enough time to finish the task. After a week, Master Grocyn examined the work I had completed and compared it with the manuscript. Immediately he began to shake his head disapprovingly. "More, this is not an exercise to be translated word by word. When you translate a work from one language to another, be more attentive to the author's thoughts than to his language. His words are not sacred; his ideas are."

"There is not sufficient time," I objected. "The term will end."

Master Grocyn seemed entirely aware of the time remaining in the term. "Will your father permit you to remain here and work on this through the summer?"

The proposal startled me, then delighted me. I realized that I had unconsciously been dreading return to London even for the summer. "If you wrote to my father . . ." My hopes suddenly inspired me. "If you reminded him that he would be relieved of the cost of transportation," I added quickly, "he might agree."

Master Groycn smiled understandingly. "The University also pays a small fee for such work by students, More. That, too, may interest your father."

Master Grocyn wrote that day a letter to my father, and my father answered much more quickly than he answered my letters. He was agreeable, he wrote, but required that my earnings be sufficient to relieve him of sending me any allowance during the summer months.

I had received one letter from Father Colet. I had answered that but had heard nothing more from him. This new development offered opportunity to write again to him, and he replied as soon as he received my letter, expressing his delight with my progress and lavishing his praise. Master Grocyn, instead of speaking compliments, demonstrated them by his interest in my work: dissatisfaction with it and multiplication of it.

When I had completed translation of the manuscript to the satisfaction of Master Grocyn, he assigned me the task of writing for him an account of my life as a page at Lambeth Palace. I began it rather slowly until I remembered the day when I had told His Grace I wished to be a writer of great books, and the memory made me realize that, at last, I was actually beginning that life. Enthusiasm filled me, and I began to write as rapidly as I could form thoughts and transcribe them. The result must have pleased Master Grocyn, for he assigned me to begin another original work and, thereafter, repeated the assignment. All this activity had the primary effect of accelerating my learning beyond that of other students and the secondary effect of forming a friendship between the Master and myself so that I looked to him for guidance and direction as well as instruction and learning.

In October of 1493, when I had been twenty months at Oxford, I became involved in one of those inconsequential arguments of schoolboys and, though satisfied as to the correctness of my statements, appealed to Master Grocyn for confirmation. Instead of answering my question, the Master told me bluntly, "More, your character lacks one important quality. You do not appreciate the superiority of your talents and, therefore, neither do others."

I did not pretend to understand him.

"Learn this, More," he said. "Being learned is good in itself but it is insufficient. Others must recognize and admit that you are learned. Argument and fact will not do that. You must develop your manner. You must conduct yourself in a manner that will show that you are yourself conscious of your superiority. That is the only way you can convince them that you are more learned than they."

"They will say that I am conceited."

"That is unimportant. They will admit that you are more learned than they."

I must have frowned as I foresaw the abuse my schoolmates would heap on me as they did on all who pretended to superiority.

"Fearful, More?" Master Grocyn taunted. "I will give you a new assignment to help you surmount your fears among the others. From this day—from this very moment—you will not again address me as 'Master.' You will address me as 'Grocyn' just as I address you as 'More.'"

The proposal made me laugh self-consciously, but he repeated it, and I picked up some work papers in order to escape. I knew that he wanted me to mold myself in imitation of him and of his manner. The thought troubled me, for I could submit myself willingly to his direction but could not presume to patronize others as he did. In that instant I realized that I had already begun to mold myself in imitation of another—that I had been exerting myself to be friendly with all others, to be interested in conversation with others. I realized that, for months, I had been forming myself to be a man similar to the Father Colet I remembered and the Father Colet who was revealed in his letters to me. I knew that, during those months, my attention at Mass had been divided between the Holy Sacrifice and whatever priest was celebrant. I did not want to be learned and patronizing as was Master Grocyn; I wanted to be learned and friendly as was Father Colet.

"How would I know if I had a vocation to the priesthood?" I asked the Master abruptly.

Master Grocyn raised his eyebrows in mock astonishment at this sudden intrusion of a new subject, but he answered without hesitation as though long familiar with it. "Most priests say they know they have a vocation only on the day of their ordination. Until then, they follow the opinion of Aquinas that it is better to solve the question by studying for the priesthood and letting the years of study constitute a trial of their vocation."

My attention wandered again from Master Grocyn, the room, the papers I still held in my hands. Imagination formed a complex that was some part myself and some part Father Colet. I could not form myself into the physical counterpart of the tall priest, but I could substitute my smaller figure and contemplate the resultant picture with some pleasure.

"In your case, More," the Master said recalling me to the present, "I should think that excellent advice."

I glanced toward him inquiringly. "That I should make trial of a vocation?"

He nodded. "No other activity affords a young man of great talent and little money such opportunity to pursue learning as the priesthood."

I felt an immediate revulsion to the cynical proposal of using the priesthood merely as a means for the pursuit of learning. Father Colet had not become a priest to pursue learning or to seek advancement. One—and only one—consideration would draw me to the priesthood, I determined: to give my mind and heart to God as had Father Colet.

6

THROUGH the remainder of that year, I wrestled with my problem without asking more questions of Grocyn. I needed and wanted advice, but his initial comment warned me against seeking it from him. I spoke to a priest, without telling that I had spoken to the Master, and he answered that I should study for the priesthood and let time resolve my doubts. I spoke to another and received the same answer. Because their answers resembled a part of Master Grocyn's statement, I did not ask other priests. I thought several times of appealing to Archbishop Morton but, before I could act, news arrived at Oxford that he was no longer Archbishop-Lord Chancellor but had become Cardinal-Lord Chancellor, and I abandoned all thought of writing to him. A mere student at Oxford could not send his problems to a Prince of the Church.

The months of turmoil and uncertainty clarified one aspect of the problem: If I were to become a priest, I would not permit any to suppose that my vocation was a subterfuge. None could say that I was entering the priesthood to advance in learning or to advance to high position in Church or state. When that was clear in my mind, I knew also that I could not study for the priesthood at Oxford with the others who aspired to parish or college life. There was but one place where I could become a priest and where

I would be protected against unfounded accusations. That was the house of the Carthusians, the Charterhouse, just outside the north wall of London. A man who entered that restricted life could never be accused of any motive other than self-sacrifice and love of God.

In December, while writing to Father Colet in far-off Rome, I revealed my thoughts to another for the first time but phrased them carefully in guarded and indirect terms. I could not permit even Father Colet to know how far they had progressed. Six weeks later I received his reply. "Your labored effort to conceal your thoughts and desires," he wrote, "are creditable neither to a student of Oxford, who should be more proficient in guile, nor to an aspirant to the Carthusian life, for which humility is a primary requisite. For this reason, alone, I should advise you against applying for entrance into the Charterhouse."

I read the stinging words over and over. It seemed incredible that Father Colet could have written them. With each reading, their injury increased. Indignantly, I tore the letter into small fragments. I put both the letter and Father Colet from my mind.

In the afternoon, when I went to Grocyn's room, I had forgotten neither priest nor letter. The sting of the words hurt as much as before. The table at which I worked was at least four inches from the most advantageous position, and I pushed it so that it scraped noisily across the floor somewhat more than the desired distance. I felt, rather than saw, Grocyn regarding me curiously.

I could not concentrate on the work before me; repeatedly I raised my eyes and stared through the window, where there was nothing more interesting than a grove of trees, bare of all foliage and unworthy of such study. The seat became uncomfortable, and I moved about so much that the chair squeaked continually.

"I have told you," Grocyn complained after a time, "to value your talents and make others value them. I did not tell you," he added caustically, "to become angry if others presumed to be your equal."

I hunched myself forward with my elbows on the table, and the chair squeaked rebelliously. I felt a perverse pleasure in Grocyn's unwitting reference to Father Colet as my equal.

With the beginning of the new year of 1494, I could suppress no longer the demand for positive action toward my objective. I began to write a letter to the Prior of the Charterhouse, but my courage failed. I needed moral support and encouragement. I had no alternative but to tell my purpose to Master Grocyn.

"You are romancing," the Master rebuked me sharply as soon as he understood. "Does the Almighty give a man a fine mind and literary talent to have him shut himself up behind the stone walls of the Charterhouse?"

For the first time since I had arrived at Oxford almost two years before, I rebelled openly and vehemently against the Master, opposing his words with words of my own. I countered his manner of superiority by ignoring it; I rejected his patronizing manner by refusing to be patronized. Inevitably, he became angry as my words and recklessness increased.

"You are verging on insolence," be warned.

"I am valuing my opinions, Grocyn," I retorted.

The familiar words and the fact that, for the first time, I had addressed him simply as "Grocyn," disconcerted him momentarily. He drew back from the belligerent position he had assumed and regarded me critically. Then he admitted defeat. "No other answer would have satisfied me," he grumbled.

My body relaxed, making me aware that I had become tense and straining while the dispute raged. A pleasant sense of achievement and victory filled me, and I smiled. Now I would be able to write to the Prior of the Charterhouse, for I had forced Grocyn to give his moral support to my purpose. I started toward the door.

"You have made me value your talent," Grocyn called after me. "But you are deluding yourself about the Charterhouse, More."

I turned angrily to face him but suppressed the words that surged into mind. I was afraid to speak. I fled from the room.

I wrote four letters that day to the Prior of the Charterhouse and destroyed each as I finished it. None were satisfactory. None expressed what I wanted to express, for I could not clearly understand my reason for applying to be admitted. Grocyn's last words had stolen from me the feeling that I had forced him to support me. At last I realized that I had still to find support and encouragement before I could advance my purpose.

Anger, hopelessness, and desperation prompted the next step. I could not continue struggling with the problem. I wrote to my father explaining the goal of my life. "Almost from the day I entered Oxford," I elaborated, "I have known what my life must be. His Eminence, the Cardinal, knew even before I did, though he was content to send me here that I might discover it for myself. My vocation is to become a priest." I paused for a long time, considering whether I should add that I wished to enter the Carthusians. I decided that the announcement of my vocation was sufficient for the present.

My father answered more promptly than was his custom. "Like many others permitted to mingle with their betters, you have been deceived with visions of greatness rising from your vast learning. I agreed to your entrance into Oxford only for reasons of respect to His Eminence; but what was tolerable before has now become unendurable. You will leave Oxford and return to London not later than next week that you may begin to read the law."

Disappointment and frustration overwhelmed me. At one stroke, I was barred from following my vocation and was also withdrawn from Oxford. I went to Grocyn for sympathy; but he read the letter, then did nothing more than sit for a long time staring at it.

"I wanted to make a great man of you, More," he said slowly. "I thought I had found a student at last of whom people would say, 'He was a pupil of Grocyn.'"

He was as disappointed as I was myself.

7

BEFORE I left Oxford, resentment supplanted disappointment. My father had opposed my entrance into the University; now he opposed my vocation to the priesthood. He had determined that, as I was his eldest son, I must put aside my own wishes, talents, and inclinations to begin the career of his choice.

My family's neighbors on Milk Street, my father's friends of the law courts, the family of my sister's husband, all welcomed me with a deference even greater than before. I was to them not only the protégé of His Eminence, the Cardinal-Lord Chancellor, but also a youth trained in the learning of Oxford. My father's attitude was restrained, as though determined to achieve his purpose yet anxious not to provoke me into rebellion. So unpleasant was my situation that I was relatively happy on the day that I began residence as a student at New Inn, just outside London.

The habit of study surmounted my antipathy toward the law. I was as one who could not refuse to learn whatever subject was thrust before him. Before the end of my first month in that school, I had received the plaudits of the Readers, as the masters were known, and began to overshadow my fellow students despite their strenuous efforts to achieve what I accomplished readily. As my ability became evident, other students sought my assistance, then my companionship. I was willing to assist—perhaps eager to demonstrate my superior talents—but I could not endure their companionship; their interests and knowledge were limited to law and legal matters, while I held steadfastly to my vocation and hungered for the delights of literature. At the end of the first month, my father came for the permitted visit and to receive a report of my progress from the Readers. Elated, he led me into the courtyard where fathers and sons enjoyed their reunions, and conducted me from group to group, finding his friends and reciting to them my accomplishments. We must have been a strange sight—a short, round, beaming father hurrying about to display his small, slight son who steadfastly refused to indicate interest or pleasure. The most interesting moment of the day for me was the time of his departure.

We walked together toward the gate opening from the courtyard, my father looking about for any friends he had not discovered previously and waving again to those he had. When we arrived at the gate and he had exhausted all possibilities, he turned his entire attention to me. "Son, now that you can see how able you are, you will find more pleasure in the law—as much, even more than I."

Perhaps because he was smiling with tremendous assurance, I found particular delight in saying to him: "I shall never like the law."

His smile did not diminish. Rather it increased, indicating his confidence that he was entirely correct. I returned to my lodgings, knowing that the day had strengthened my determination to realize my vocation.

For some months, my father came regularly to see me, but I maintained such a reserve and indicated such a lack of interest that, at last, I began to discourage him. Before the end of the first term, he was satisfied to obtain the progress report from the Readers, speak with me for a few minutes, and return to London. I found both companionship and pleasure in writing long letters, which were true literary efforts, to Grocyn, and receiving equally long letters from him.

In 1496, when I was eighteen and had exhausted the educational resources of the Readers at New Inn, I was entered at Lincoln's Inn, reputed to be the most stringent and demanding. The most notable circumstance of that day of transfer was the location of the lodgings to which I was assigned. From the window of my room, I had an unobstructed view of the Charterhouse. As though the circumstance was an omen of progress toward my goal, my spirits lifted appreciably for the first time since my departure from Oxford. I wrote immediately to Grocyn, told him of my transfer and the reason for it, and, disdainful of his opinion, commented at length on the Charterhouse, its situation, its mass of gray stone surmounted by tiling that reflected the early morning sun. In return, Grocyn complimented me on the evident manner of superiority I had assumed to myself. "Though I will tell you, More," he added, "that you need not endeavor to exercise it against me. I have already expressed myself as to the stupidity of entombing talents in such a place as the Charterhouse and trust you will not discredit me by pursuing such an objective. Even though you shall become a lawyer, the excess of your literary talent is such that you can yet be a source of pride to me." I laughed at the peculiar and individual manner in which Grocyn had complimented my talents; but I got also a feeling of delight from reading his perfectly composed letter.

A series of minor incidents stemmed directly from my optimism that mere sight of the Charterhouse assured me of eventual achievement of that goal. I was freed from the necessity of concentrating attention on my purpose and imbued with greater interest in the problems of law. Within a short time, I achieved even greater distinction as a student at Lincoln's than I had enjoyed at New Inn. This generated a proportionate degree of delight in my father, who now fairly reveled in my progress reports. My disposition also improved; I was more pleasant to my father, and he began to lengthen his visits with me.

Some part of my attitude was the result of deliberate planning, for I began at that same time to engage in writing which, in addition to the long letters to Grocyn, necessitated much greater expenditures for paper and writing materials. An increased allowance was imperative, and I was quite willing that my father enjoy my accomplishments if he were willing also to support my literary activities. I disliked the law no less than before, but I learned to use it for my own purpose and obtained an increased allowance from him.

Perhaps this incident marked my discovery of the disparity between my father's talents and my own. He was older than my schoolmates, whom I regarded as of little learning and less intelligence, yet he was representative of them whose company I avoided.

Such association as I permitted myself with the other students was restricted to discussions among the groups that gathered in the courtyard, when the weather was agreeable, or in the students' common room at other times. There, with the advantage of my Oxford training, I found a perverse pleasure in forcing others to recognize my superiority and silencing any adversaries. I regarded my lack of sympathy with their aims and interests as further proof that I was not of the world—at least of the legal world.

I had completed one year at Lincoln's when the Parliament of 1497 voted a grant of £83,000 to King Henry VII for war against King James of Scotland, and provided a tax levy for accumulating that great sum. The people of London complained among themselves, bewailing the necessity of paying for war. Within a week, their plaints turned suddenly to cries of anger against the Lord Chancellor, Cardinal Morton. The same phenomena occurred in the common room of Lincoln's, where the grant and the tax were discussed by my fellow students. Discussions were limited, in the beginning, to the grant, the tax, and the necessity for war, then suddenly turned to denunciation of the Cardinal.

I was present on a morning when one student, gifted in oratory, had attracted a large number about him while he fulminated against the Cardinal-Lord Chancellor, then permitted himself to expand his attack until he included all clergy in the service of King Henry. What he lacked of knowledge he provided with talent. "They stand between the people and the King, crushing the one as they usurp the power of the other. None may live but to serve them. None may eat until they are fed." In this manner he continued for some time, returning at last to Cardinal Morton as leader and archcriminal of all.

"You are ignorant," I called to him when I could endure no more.

So quietly had the crowd of students been listening that he had not expected opposition. He was opening his mouth for some statement of his own when my interruption distracted him. His mouth closed and his arms fell while he looked over the crowd for the one who had spoken. Other students also turned round.

"You are ignorant," I repeated, so that he would know who had interrupted him. "You blame Cardinal Morton for a war that King James started. You blame Cardinal Morton for a tax imposed by the Parliament. You would blame every ill of poverty and sickness on him, too."

"You have your own reasons for defending the Lord Chancellor, Master More," he charged quickly. The crowd rumbled appreciation of his thrust. "Not everyone is privileged to enter Oxford," he added crudely.

"That would require more brains than tongue," I taunted.

"And the favor of the Lord Chancellor," he answered. The students around us roared approval. Some of them jeered.

I realized that I was near defeat even before I had an opportunity to be heard and to defend the Cardinal. In that realization, I happened on the explanation of the Londoners' cries against my patron and the antagonism of my school fellows toward the Lord Chancellor. I remembered the Cardinal's own comment to my father and rephrased it now for my own use. "Lawyers' envy!" I shouted. "You covet service with the King. You envy the Cardinal and the clergy because you covet their positions! You spread lies against the Cardinal and the clergy to turn the people against them!"

"Let the clergy attend to matters of the Church. Let lawyers attend to matters of state," my opponent shouted in return.

"There would be no state were it not for the clergy," I retorted. "There would be no lawyers were it not for the clergy who . . ." The crowd of students roared a protest so loudly that I could not be heard. I waited until they quieted.

"Neither you nor the people of London would complain against His Grace except for lawyers who tell you to complain against him. Why? Because lawyers fear to complain against the King. You have not the courage to complain against the King—just as the King has so little courage he must hide behind the Cardinal's robes."

For a moment, the crowd was silent. There was some faint chance that I might still persuade them to my views. My opponent must also have recognized the slight indication of favor I had won.

"Men have been executed for treason who have said less than you, Master More," he warned.

The tone of his voice made me pause. He had become furiously angry. His face was pale. He had not spoken his words as a warning; he had spoken them as a threat to report my words to the King's men. He saw the imminence of defeat and humiliation and would use whatever device he could to avoid them.

Some portion of prudence restrained me. I remembered some who had barely escaped death for lesser offenses. I remembered others who had not escaped and whose bodies had been torn apart at Tyburn. I remembered that the Earl of Warwick was in the Tower for no greater crime than the royal blood in his veins. I was acutely aware that King Henry had won his throne by force and would use force without hesitation for any end. I dared not speak again; I turned away and left the room.

I walked into London slowly and without purpose, other than to separate myself physically from those from whom I was separated by divergent interests. Loyalty to the Cardinal alone did not account for my defense of him and the clergy. Neither had I simply involved myself in argument to subdue an opponent, as I had on other occasions. My initial interruption had sprung from my vocation, which made me one with all priests, whom I must defend as I would defend myself. Something more, too, had prompted me to reckless-ness—that hatred of law which had remained as constant as my determination to the priesthood.

I had entered the city and arrived at St. Paul's when the last of these elements became clear to me. I turned north, on sudden impulse, hurrying along the crowded streets, through the north wall, and arrived before the Charter-house. I could delay no longer.

8

FATHER Paul received me. He was a ruddy-faced, deep-chested man of medium height who led me energetically from the outer gate, across a small, enclosed courtyard and through the doorway of the Charterhouse. Inside the building, he guided me through a semidark entranceway and into a room furnished with a single table and six chairs. Through the window, I could see the garden we had just crossed and the outer gate.

"Our reception room, Master More," Father Paul informed me. He took one of the chairs by the window for himself and indicated that I should occupy the other. "Now, Master More, how can I assist you?"

"I think I should speak with the Prior," I told him hesitantly. "I wish to apply for admission." My carefully cultivated manner of assurance and superiority had deserted me in these strange surroundings.

Father Paul smiled, moved his head first in agreement, then in disagreement. "You seem rather young, Master More. What is your age?"

"Nineteen."

Father Paul offered no comment about my age. He digressed from that subject to tell me the history of the Carthusians and the purpose of the order. He came at last to enumerating the requirements for entrance and, in this manner, informed me that I must wait patiently until I was at least twenty unless I might offer some unusual reason which would justify admission before that time.

I gained from that first visit nothing more than an intense liking for this energetic priest and the impression that he liked me in return. "Return whenever you wish, Master More," he told me at departure. "I shall be glad to see you whenever you come." His friendliness and interest counterbalanced my disappointment. I had now, in addition to my literary efforts and my correspondence with Grocyn, this third interest: friendship with Father Paul. With those three to claim my attention I succeeded in avoiding other arguments with my fellow students at law school.

I visited Father Paul several times before I discovered that he was a man of extraordinary but specialized learning. He could quote at great length from Scripture and from the writings of the Holy Fathers but, when I mentioned those authors of ancient Greece and Rome, whose writings Grocyn had taught me to love, he revealed both ignorance and disinterest.

"Life, Master More," he explained one day, "has meaning only when it is related to death. Those authors you love avoid all reference to the meaning of either life or death, so they are unimportant." I would have disagreed vehemently had any other so dismissed those great names, but Father Paul's manner of expression aroused no resentment. He spoke as though he wished only to explain his lack of interest and not with the intention of criticizing me.

As my twentieth birthday approached, I reminded him that I should soon be able to comply with that requirement. Soon after, I received a note from him that I should present myself at the Charterhouse on the day of my birthday, when

Prior William would speak with me. I felt that my goal was within my grasp at last.

Father Paul led me into the reception room and waited to present me to Prior William. I expected him to remain during my interview and was dismayed when he withdrew, leaving me to state my case to the Prior without the benefit of his prompting. I was, in fact, more conscious of my need for him at the moment he departed than I had been before, for Prior William was a reserved, unsmiling man who seemed little interested in acquiring a new member for his community. When we sat in the chairs at the window, he did not relax as did Father Paul, but held himself upright as though impatient for the interview to come quickly to an end.

"Father Paul has informed me of your desire to enter the Charterhouse, Master More." He spoke softly but very rapidly. "Tell me about your vocation."

For a moment, his invitation unbalanced me. I had not arranged my thoughts in order. I expected that he would ask a few formal questions, then grant me admission. However, I realized quickly that his invitation afforded me the opportunity of offsetting his apparent lack of interest in me as a candidate and that I might now present sufficient information that would elicit an actual invitation from him to enter the Community. I told, very briefly, of my initial desire to imitate Father Colet but of my unwillingness to permit any to say that I was entering the priesthood for my own advancement.

"Do the opinions of others trouble you, Master More?" he asked then.

"I would not give any the opportunity to degrade the priesthood by saying that I entered it for an unworthy motive," I explained.

"So you selected the Carthusians," he prompted.

"That all would know I was prompted by the love of God," I agreed quickly.

"Continue, Master More."

I had become aware that his eyes were very black and quite small and that he held them steadily on me. My confidence began to deteriorate; it was imperative that I relate my accomplishments and talents as much to restore my assurance as to impress him. I related at length my progress in law, despite my dislike for it, my literary interests and ability, conveying in this manner an impression of the career I might enjoy and which I was willing to sacrifice. I included, as a matter of course, my regular reception of the sacraments and attendance at devotions. I was encouraged, as I progressed, by a slight smile.

"You do have extraordinary talents, Master More," he remarked when I had finished, "but I am not at all sure that they are such talents as God desires in the Charterhouse. You seem more fitted to the active life than to the contemplative. I am afraid that a creative writer, as you seem destined to be, would tire if I assigned him to copy Sacred Scripture or the Missal."

"Soon you will print those, Prior William," I smiled.

He nodded agreement. "When that day comes, Master More, we will devote more time to prayer and will reduce our activities to more menial tasks. When there is no longer need to copy and illustrate, the Community can apply itself more diligently to prayer and penance."

The prospect of regular prayer and penance which his words suggested momentarily silenced me. For the first time, I felt uncertain. "Does not every member of the Community have to adjust himself to the life, Prior William?"

"To some extent, Master More, and some more than others. For many, such an adjustment is impossible."

I understood that he regarded me as among the "many" rather than the "some." "Surely, Prior William, I have not cherished my vocation all these years if it is nothing more than an illusion?" I demanded.

"Not at all, Master More. You may indeed have a vocation. I hope I do not offend you by expressing a doubt that you have a vocation to the Carthusian life."

"You could permit me a period of trial," I proposed.

He turned his eyes from me as though embarrassed by my insistence and the necessity I was forcing on him of refusing me completely. "I am always hesitant, Master More, to refuse a man completely," he said finally. "On some occasions in the past, other candidates have disagreed with me as you are doing. I will agree with you as I agreed with them. You may prove your vocation to this life by living here in the guesthouse for a time."

"But that would require some income, Prior William," I objected. "I should need at least sufficient to provide my own clothing."

He stood up slowly to end our discussion. "If God wants you to enter this life, Master More, He will provide the means."

For a short time, I was thoroughly dejected by the result of the interview. I had held so long and so tenaciously to my idea that Prior William's decision seemed arbitrary. I saw the hopelessness of seeking another interview to persuade him to my view. I plunged wholeheartedly into prayer, realizing that I had exhausted my own resources.

I did not pray after the manner of our blessed Lord— "not my will but thine." I was convinced that I was destined to the Carthusian life, and I prayed only for the means of realizing that destiny. I prayed less that I might enter the Charterhouse, and more that God would provide the means by which I should be enabled to enter. As the months of 1498 passed and I approached my twenty-first birthday, on which I should receive my certificate as a lawyer, I prayed with increasing desperation.

9

AT the close of a lecture period, early in January of 1499, I was summoned to the office of the Proctor of Lincoln's. The presence of my father and two other gentlemen suggested that I had been called to receive some new honor; my father's expression of paternal pride and self-satisfaction certainly contributed to that impression. However, when I was presented to the two strangers I learned that they represented Furnivall's Inn, a law school esteemed somewhat midway between New Inn and Lincoln's. Whatever the reason for the summons, I was curious rather than interested since it would pertain to the law, and my mind was completely engaged with the problem of admission into the Charterhouse.

"Master More," one of the strangers explained when we were seated, "your name entered, either accidentally or fortuitously, into certain discussions we have had with your revered proctor." He bowed ceremoniously to Proctor Winton, who returned his bow with equal gravity. "We of Furnivall's consulted with your revered proctor"—the bowing ceremony was repeated—"seeking his advice in a matter pertaining to a position of reader that is now vacant at Furnivall's."

My mind veered into comparison of the formal, exaggerated, ceremonious bowing of the two men with the simple, unaffected, truly respectful attitudes of Prior William and Father Paul. The actions of these two lawyers were nothing greater than fatuous and shallow ceremony; those of the two priests were based on a feeling of common brotherhood. I listened apathetically while the stranger continued his long monologue, interrupted with frequent bows to the "revered Proctor" or to his "honored colleague" or to my "beloved father" or to me whom he termed a "most talented young man." His complex and ambiguous manner of offering me the position of Reader at Furnivall's annoyed me—the very thought of becoming involved in the teaching of the law revolted me. I wanted to turn and escape from the group. "I have had no practical experience," I objected when he seemed to desire an answer.

"You need none, Thomas," my father interjected quickly. "The position of Reader requires more a man acquainted with theory than one fortified by experience." He leaned back in his chair but immediately bent forward again. "The position provides an income of £25 for each term. What other young lawyer can look forward to such an income immediately on receiving his certificate?"

My mind had been busily searching for new excuses while my father spoke. His words penetrated sufficiently to make me understand all that this offer constituted. I was shocked by the realization that I had almost rejected the means God was providing for the attainment of my own objective. I knew that neither the Proctor nor my father nor the other two attributed this opportunity to any cause other than my own accomplishments at Lincoln and my evident superiority over my schoolmates. I believed myself that this was God's manner of answering my prayers and a certain sign of His pleasure that I enter the Charterhouse. I smiled at my father, at the Proctor, and at the other two waiting for my answer, preparing them for sudden reversal of my attitude. "I hope I shall justify your confidence," and I bowed ceremoniously. As soon as I could free myself from them, I rushed to announce this measure of Divine Providence to Father Paul.

The final month at Lincoln's was an ordeal more painful than all the five years since I had been withdrawn from Oxford. Several times I began letters to Grocyn but abandoned each effort. I tried to distract myself with translations, but that also failed. I offered grateful prayers to God for the manner He had answered my petition, and in that alone was I able to concentrate successfully.

Preoccupied as I was during that final month, I gave little consideration to the events of my birthday other than that of receiving the certificate which would enable me to realize my purpose. On that day I could think only of the moment when I should arrive at the Charterhouse. Thus, the ceremonies accompanying the bestowal of my certificate were distasteful. I was not prepared to endure the congratulations of Proctor Winton and the readers gathered for the ceremony. Certainly, I had not prepared for my father's presence, his expansive conceit, his boasts, and his company.

When the ordeal ended, I hurried from the room, intent on my purpose. My father hurried after me.

"You are walking too fast, son," he complained when we had passed through the gate from the courtyard.

"I have a purpose in life now," I answered grimly. I slowed my pace because the countryside itself suggested the plan I should follow. Ahead of us was the west wall of the city. Immediately before the gate, a road branched to the left to pass the city on the north. It was this road I would walk to the Charterhouse. At the junction, therefore, I would announce my destination.

My father amused himself with his aimless chatter intended to amuse me. I answered sufficiently often to avoid warning him that the situation was not as pleasant as he thought it to be. When I stopped, therefore, at the junction of the roads, he regarded me questioningly, the smile of satisfaction still on his face.

"I will leave you here," I announced briskly. "I am going to the Charterhouse."

Surprise and curiosity reduced his smile. "Will you be there long?" he asked innocently.

"I will be there forever," I answered bluntly. "I will enter the Carthusians and become a priest."

Astonishment replaced his expression of pleasure. "You are a lawyer—you agreed to be a reader at Furnivall's," he protested.

I smiled with the feeling of pleasure in my victory over all the obstacles I had surmounted. "I will be reader for a time. That will support me while I live in the guesthouse until I can enter the community."

My explanation seemed only to increase his bewilderment. "You are trained for the law—not for the priesthood."

"I am trained for the law because you removed me from Oxford and made me train for the law," I retorted coldly. "Now I am of age, I am independent. I will train now for the priesthood." I did not want to argue and contend with him. The necessity for that had ended. But he stood quite still, and I could not simply walk away from him.

"Did you allow me to support you through law school?" he demanded indignantly. "Did you permit me to spend all that money when you had no intention of practicing law?" As he understood my purpose, he became angry.

I wanted to quiet him but I could not abandon my own goal. "I told you long ago," I reminded, "that I wanted to become a priest."

"You had no priestly vocation," he exclaimed.

"You would not permit me to remain at Oxford while I tested my vocation."

"You never said more about it," he accused. "You seemed content with the law."

"I seemed content with the law because you demanded that I either study law or cease learning altogether. Had I said more about the priesthood, you would have withdrawn me from law school and put me into service as secretary or clerk to some of the great." The memory of the past flooded back and overwhelmed my intention not to become angry. "You interfered with my vocation once. I would not give you opportunity to interfere with it again."

His indignation seemed to disappear. I saw some indication of fear in his attitude.

I seized the opportunity for increasing his fear. "Almighty God had a purpose for me quite different from yours." I turned away; I realized that my anger was overpowering me. Without looking back, I walked quickly along the road to the Charterhouse.

Father Paul was not available, but the brother who admitted me had been informed of my arrival. I was relieved that I need not meet Father Paul immediately; the dispute with my father had disturbed me, and I was afraid that the priest would inquire the cause of my troubled manner. The brother exhibited no interest in me other than to lead me through the corridors and stairways of the guesthouse, to the small room assigned to me.

I had at my disposal a bed along one wall, a table beneath the window, and a single chair. A crucifix was fastened to the wall above the bed. Pegs in the opposite wall suggested a place for my clothing. The most interesting feature of the room was the view from the window, for this room, on the third story, overlooked the individual cells of the monks and their gardens. Prior William probably had assigned me the room that I would be able to see, if not participate in, the life I desired.

Nothing would dissuade or discourage me, I determined fiercely. Father Colet, Master Grocyn, my father, Prior William—all would learn their mistake in time. I would fix all my efforts, all my desire, all my energies to this future. I would begin now to adjust myself to this life. My thoughts went far into the future. I saw the necessity for incessant effort beyond the period of adjustment. "I will be a saint," I determined. "I will be a saint as all these Carthusians are saints, and men will revere my memory."

10

SANCTITY! The thought was as staggering as it was pleasant. It helped to eliminate from my mind the last remnant of disturbance remaining from the dispute with my father. I turned away from the window and stretched out on the bed the better to contemplate my purpose. Some time passed before I realized that I was not contemplating but was idly dreaming of St. Paul and St. Thomas of Canterbury. Dedication to sanctity would demand more of me than this. I must plan. I must have a program for the cultivation and development of my new life. Resolutely I rolled from the bed. I had brought no paper with me, and now I needed paper for the project I had in mind. I tried the drawer of the table.

Paper was there, but it was not what I sought. It was a part of a manuscript, many pages of which were missing and many others damaged. Evidently it had been consulted often by those who had occupied this room before me.

> "Behold, Almighty God, with Thy accustomed patience, how carefully we respect the conventional rules of spelling and grammar, received from men, yet neglect the rules of eternal salvation, received from Thee."

I thrilled with my discovery. Here was an unknown who revealed at once the love of learning, love of God, and love of letters in which I reveled.

> "How scrupulously we avoid grammatical error even when, with hatred and savage eloquence, we denounce our fellow man."

I read on, cringing interiorly at times as the unknown author tabulated his crimes, reminding me that I was also a criminal in the sight of God. Then I rejoiced as the author extolled the great mercy of God. I was entranced in reading the fragment of manuscript when Father Paul came for his first visit to me.

Father Paul laughed when I asked identification of the manuscript. "Are you the learned Master More," he mocked, "but do not recognize the *Confessions* of St. Augustine?"

"I never had cause to read anything of St. Augustine. I thought . . ." I began but stopped before I should give Father Paul new reason to mock me.

He laughed longer than before. "You thought St. Augustine wrote great heavy works in vile phrasing that you could not read with either pleasure or profit." He handed the manuscript back to me. "Don't be disturbed. I think we must all discover by accident the writings of the Holy Doctors before we will believe that they are interesting. But, now that you have discovered the great bishop, why does he interest you?"

I read to him the parts that had attracted me to the manuscript. "I was looking for paper," I explained, "when I discovered this. I wanted paper to plan a new life for myself. I know now that I need more than paper. I need instruction, and I want to read the rest of this for what instruction I can derive from it."

"Some of his other works afford more instruction," Father Paul proposed. I may have revealed some impatience, for he continued quickly, "but, if this interests you, by all means read this first."

"I didn't intend to discount your suggestion," I apologized. "I wanted to discover what this author did to develop the spirit."

"What did our blessed Lord do?" Father Paul challenged.

"He went into the desert." I faltered because my mind was not accustomed to reciting the activities of our Lord in precise order. "He fasted for forty days in the desert . . ."

"You will not find better example nor hear better advice."

"What else shall I do?"

"'The purpose of the virtuous man depends not on his wisdom but on God's grace, and he relies on God's help for its accomplishment.' Those are not my words, Master More. They are the words of Thomas à Kempis. Do they indicate what you should do besides fasting?"

"Pray?"

"Without ceasing," Father Paul exclaimed emphatically. "Without constant prayer, even fasting and mortification may become an enemy and a danger to us."

"After that?" I suggested.

Father Paul smiled and shook his head. "You must learn first to walk in God's ways and in His service before you can run. You must first train and strengthen your muscles. Be content for the present with prayer and fasting—the life of the spirit is born from the death of the flesh."

I began a new manner of life that day. Father Paul outlined for me what fasting I should do and the mortifications I should practice. For prayer, he required principally that

I be present at the hours when the community gathered in the church to sing the office. I put my father from my mind; his attitude had shown that he could not understand this life I desired. I could not undertake the task of convincing him against the force of his own desires.

*   *   *   *   *

At Furnivall's the initial attitude of the students, the other readers, and those in charge of the school strengthened this resolve. They seemed to have learned immediately of my new residence and new manner of life; I felt a spirit of animosity on the part of both superiors and students from the very beginning. Lawyers and student lawyers necessarily looked with suspicion on one who deserted their ranks to number himself with the clergy. I was not concerned. I had my contract as reader; I was the outstanding student of Lincoln's. They could not so soon terminate my contract without admitting foolishness in having employed me; they could not readily find another of equal learning.

Father Paul brought me a complete copy of the *Confessions,* and I devoured it. My enthusiasm mounted. The learning of the great bishop far exceeded my most exaggerated hopes for my own learning in the future. Here was a man I could respect, one I could follow and imitate. Here, too, was a man who expressed tremendous thoughts in flawless language as pure as the style of those pagan and profane authors I loved. When I finished the *Confessions,* I wrote a long letter to Grocyn, describing my discovery enthusiastically, letting that enthusiasm overshadow whatever effect the announcement of my new life might have on him.

"Your announcement provokes and irritates me," Grocyn answered, "but it seems to have served one useful purpose already if it has caused you to discover literature which I could not bring to your attention because of your youth while you were at Oxford. I cannot share your enthusiasm for St. Augustine, as I confess he is interested in a degree of spirituality that fails to attract me. However, you will have ample opportunity to indulge your great enthusiasm to satiety if you will receive and entertain a man to whom I have recommended you. I have learned recently that Erasmus of Rotterdam, a great scholar of Europe, will arrive in England in June. I know he will visit you because I included your name among those I gave him as worthy of visiting when he arrives in London; and I emphasized that you were most proficient of all in both literature and the Latin tongue. This last is most important to him, as he has no knowledge of English and must speak either in his native tongue, in Greek, or in Latin. Of these, he prefers Latin. Erasmus, like you, extols the literary perfection of St. Augustine and is completely familiar with all of his works.

"You will be interested that our mutual friend, Colet, has returned from the Continent. I was quite surprised to learn that you have not continued your correspondence with him."

His reference to Father Colet annoyed me. I had said nothing to Grocyn of my letter to the priest or his answer; but the Master had ample opportunity to discern that I had set Father Colet apart from my interests. His words about the unknown Erasmus more than compensated, however, and it occurred to me that he had joined the two names in one letter as I had joined praise of St. Augustine to the announcement of my entrance into the Carthusians. I laughed then to realize how much I had appropriated to myself of Grocyn's manner.

Immediately, I obtained additional works of St. Augustine from Father Paul to prepare for the coming of Erasmus. I applied to them every minute not demanded by my contract with Furnivall's or by my life at the Charterhouse, and finished reading them in a relatively short time. When I returned them to Father Paul and requested others, he became reluctant.

"You are not studying and considering what St. Augustine wrote," he commented. "You are reading him as you would read any author—merely for the pleasure you derive. These works were written for a man's spiritual advancement, Master More, not as mere opportunities for pleasure."

"They will not harm me," I countered, "if I read them for one purpose more than another. I fast, I mortify myself, I pray as you instructed. May I not enjoy even reading—especially the works of St. Augustine?"

11

BEFORE Erasmus arrived in June, I had read all those works of the holy bishop contained in the library of the Charterhouse. An hour after his arrival, I almost regretted that I had expended so much energy to acquire knowledge of St. Augustine in such a short time. I had not consciously constructed an image of the man I expected to meet—I knew nothing of his appearance—but, perhaps misled subconsciously by Grocyn's bulkiness and Father Colet's manliness, I was not prepared for the plaintive softness and affectations of Erasmus.

He was slightly taller than I but more slender. He was thirty-three, twelve years my senior, but his comportment created immediately an impression of immaturity. His conversation sparkled with wit, his observations revealed a learning far exceeding Grocyn's, but his high-pitched voice and expression bordered on the effeminate. During the Saturday and Sunday I devoted to his entertainment, I was alternately delighted by his mind and repelled by his mannerisms. When Erasmus departed for Oxford, I was relieved with the knowledge that I had successfully discharged my obligations to entertain him. Having lived nine years in a completely masculine environment, and living now amid the intense masculinity of the Charterhouse, I could not adjust myself to Erasmus.

One great benefit resulted from the experience. I was so disappointed that I renewed my resolutions that same night. On the next day, I sought Father Paul to obtain for me the works of St. Augustine that I might read them again, not for pleasure, but for spiritual profit. I intensified also my objectives of prayer, fasting and mortification.

A letter arrived soon after from Erasmus expressing his gratitude in extravagant terms. I discarded it without answering, hopeful that it ended the incident. I was surprised to receive also a letter from Father Colet, congratulating me and wishing me well in my new life. Remembering his previous words, I discarded his letter also without answering him. I was more interested in a letter from Grocyn, who referred to Erasmus in careful terms that informed me, nonetheless, that he had been as disappointed as I in the scholar's mannerisms. Other letters from Erasmus followed at short intervals, but I ignored all until he wrote such a letter that to continue silence would have been insulting to him and to Grocyn.

Shortly before the end of that year, 1499, when my period of lecturing at Furnivall's had ended for the day and I was walking across the courtyard toward the entrance gate, I was surprised and delighted when I saw a familiar, bulky figure standing just within the entrance. Grocyn! Five years had passed since I had last seen him at Oxford, but I could not mistake him. I was running toward him before he discovered me.

"More! More!" He embraced me impulsively with both arms. The unexpected display of affection startled me, then incited an equal surge of affection within me.

"Grocyn! I will not listen to you until you agree that you will stay with me during the Christmas vacation period!

Agree, Grocyn! Agree!" I drew back from him sufficiently to enable him to speak.

He laughed in a manner that indicated neither agreement nor disagreement. He was accustomed from his years of lecturing to such situations as I was thrusting on him. "I am fifty-four, More," he laughed. The comment puzzled me as he intended it should. He waited a moment for confusion to diminish my enthusiasm. "A man of fifty-four would not find comfort nor would he be admitted to the Charterhouse." I tried to protest, but he interrupted me. "I have lodgings of my own in London, More, by the kindness of His Highness, King Henry."

"You will come with me," I insisted. I gripped his arm and turned him about to start walking toward the Charterhouse.

"More!" he protested, "I have duties to perform in return for my lodgings. My residence is now the rectory of the Church of St. Lawrence, and I cannot absent myself overnight without leaving notice."

I released him as I began to realize the import of his announcement. "You are to be in London permanently?"

He smiled his self-satisfaction. "So long as I please His Highness, I shall reside permanently in London."

A tremendous happiness surged through me as I contemplated the prospect of having him near at hand, where I could talk freely with him instead of being limited by the difficulties of correspondence. I realized, too, that our relations would be the more pleasant because I was also a man and no longer the sixteen-year-old boy who had labored in his room at Oxford.

He had no objections to walking with me as far as the Charterhouse, and we expended our first enthusiasm and delight. We had turned into the road leading north around the city when Grocyn asked about my study of St. Augustine, giving me an excuse to launch an enthusiastic recital of the great bishop's learning and writings.

"More," he interrupted me after a time, "you have convinced me of the superiority of your talents. Please pause for a moment that I may tell you why I asked about St. Augustine."

"You had some reason other than politeness?" I laughed.

"A very good reason, More. I wish you to prepare a series of lectures on St. Augustine and deliver them in the Church of St. Lawrence."

The proposal astonished me. "I have never lectured on subjects of that sort."

"I did not ask whether you had lectured on that subject. I proposed that you will."

"But a scholar like Erasmus would be the proper man for that," I protested.

Grocyn made a sound indicative of disgust. "Does Grocyn's pupil now make public announcement that Erasmus is his superior in talent and learning?" he demanded.

I suspected that relations between Grocyn and Erasmus were not friendly. I realized too, that I was glad of the discovery, as though the arrival of Erasmus as Grocyn's guest had, in some manner, infringed rights I had regarded as my own. I knew, also, that Grocyn wanted to display me as his pupil. "Not at all," I answered quickly. "Outline what you want me to do."

"Prepare six lectures," Grocyn stipulated in the tone he had used to direct my work at Oxford. "Review them with me. I will arrange that the proper people will be present when you are prepared to deliver them."

I selected St. Augustine's *City of God* for my lectures rather than his works in general. Again, then, I went to Father Paul to ask him for the library manuscript. The request demanded an explanation about the lectures I must prepare and a longer explanation of Grocyn. Father Paul disapproved the project on which I was beginning and indicated some displeasure with my enthusiastic description of Grocyn. "Master More, you must soon decide whether you are interested in the life of learning or the life of a Carthusian." He did not seem to desire an answer and, though his words troubled me at the time, I forgot them completely as I prepared my lectures.

12

GROCYN gathered an audience of something more than a hundred, most of them clergy, for my first lecture at the beginning of March. I was somewhat nervous when I started, uncomfortably aware that I was a layman in the strange position of speaking to priests, but Grocyn's assurances and my experience as reader at Furnivall's supported me during the first minutes. Then I saw that those before me listened willingly, interested in my statements rather than my appearance. As I proceeded, I knew that I spoke very well. When that lecture ended and I retired to the rectory with Grocyn, I was delighted that almost all of the audience came to the rectory to compliment me.

The compliments flattered me and encouraged me so that I mounted the pulpit for the second lecture with much greater confidence. That night, many more priests were present to hear me, and I experienced real pleasure in my role. In the rectory, also, I received as many more compliments.

So well did the course of lectures progress that, at the end, several hundred attended, and I felt some disappointment that the lectures and my moment of glory had ended. I expected—and I am sure my expectations would have been fulfilled—that I should now be forgotten or but lightly remembered as the young man well acquainted with the works of St. Augustine.

Immediately following conclusion of the lectures, however, my old patron, Cardinal Morton, died. Grocyn's position as a scholar, holding a grant from the King, enabled him to obtain place for himself and for me in that section of Westminster Abbey reserved to the great of London. All seemed to know Grocyn, and he seemed to know all those surrounding us, though he conducted himself toward all with the same patronizing manner that he had displayed toward Colet and me when I had first met him. When he presented me to these great people, he mentioned my lectures in the Church of St. Lawrence but mentioned also that I had been his pupil at Oxford.

I was both puzzled and flattered by the manner in which these people received me. Few if any of them had heard my lectures, yet all referred to them as though they had received full reports about them. Many of them also referred to my residence in the Charterhouse and to my position as reader at Furnivall's. I felt a pleasant expansiveness. I was made to recognize my status in their minds as the learned young lecturer of St. Lawrence, the pious young man of the Charterhouse, and the talented reader of the law at Furnivall's. I realized with delight that all London had become aware of a young man, one Thomas More.

Immediately after, Grocyn began to meet me regularly at the conclusion of lecture periods at Furnivall's, bringing invitations to dinners and receptions at the homes of these great. I had never been conscious of latent social graces, of wit or conversational ability, and I was silent and self-conscious in the beginning. Very quickly, I became accustomed to this new experience of life and began to take active part in conversation with the others. Invitations increased rapidly, being delivered to me no longer through Grocyn, as though I were dependent on him, but by uniformed servants who brought them to me at Furnivall's.

From this social activity, a material benefit evolved in that these new and powerful friends urged some of their legal matters on me; and I, who had protested utmost dislike for law and especially for active practice in the courts, derived new pleasure from representing these clients. By the time of my twenty-third birthday, in 1501, I was firmly established as a celebrity in London. To such extent did I enjoy my success that, very generously, I resumed correspondence with Colet, who answered immediately.

Several times during this period, Father Paul objected to my activities, and I endeavored to avoid occasions that might give him more opportunities for objections. Soon after the close of the school term in 1501, Grocyn brought an invitation to visit friends of his at their home in the country. As an extended absence required permission, I was forced to approach Father Paul, despite expectation that he would seize the opportunity to express disapproval again of my activities. He turned his head slowly and resignedly from side to side as though to satisfy himself with a mute gesture instead of words that had already proved ineffective. "I cannot give you permission. I will ask Prior William if you may go."

Had I been able to invent some excuse, I should gladly have withdrawn my request. Asking Father Paul had required courage; I did not anticipate that the matter would be referred to the Prior.

I had returned to my room the following Sunday morning after Mass when a brother brought me a summons to present myself to Prior William in the reception room. I felt a premonition that the session would be unpleasant and had a feeling of guilt that I had not been pursuing my principal objective as diligently as I should. In the reception room, however, I pretended confidence and relaxed carefully in my chair.

"Father Paul has told me of your request to be absent for two weeks from the Charterhouse, Master More. Who is the family you will visit?"

"Master Nicholas Colt at Newhall in Essex," I answered readily, relieved that the Prior's interest seemed to be directed to the family of our host.

"Why do you wish to visit them?"

I was uncomfortably aware of the black eyes that observed every slight change of expression, his attention that noted every nuance of voice. I cast about for some plausible answer to an unanswerable question. I could not say why I wished to visit the Colts or to visit any of those whose invitations I had accepted in London. "They have invited me through Master Grocyn," I explained.

Prior William did not indicate whether or not the answer satisfied him. "You have been here at the Charterhouse something more than two years now?"

I nodded silently. I had found in my own short experience in the courts that those witnesses who spoke least were the most difficult to interrogate.

"What is your own evaluation of your vocation, Master More?" the Prior asked bluntly.

I felt my body tensing as I endeavored to phrase an answer that would satisfy the Prior without condemning myself. "I have been following Father Paul's directions as to fasting and prayer, Reverend Prior. I am sorry that I have not been able to make as much progress as I expected."

"Are your outside activities interfering with that?"

"Father Paul has suggested that I discontinue some of them. But Reverend Prior," I began to plead, "it seems to me that I am doing something valuable by my activities. Almost all lawyers are known to be damaging the clergy because of their envy of those priests in the service of the King. While I live here, I am identified with the clergy and yet I am also a lawyer; so my activities offset the influence of those lawyers who oppose the clergy. There is proof of that," I added, "in that the lawyers I encounter in the courts avoid me."

Prior William seemed unimpressed by my plea; but he did not pursue the questioning. We talked for a time, and I understood that he was not satisfied with my social and legal activities but would not prohibit continuation of them.

I was vaguely troubled when he granted the permission I sought, and I returned to my room. I had made no progress toward actual entrance into the community, and that was, in itself, retrogression. I was following Father Paul's directions as to fasting and mortification, but my outside activities caused more frequent absences when the Divine Office was being chanted and shortened the time available for prayer. I began to realize, without clearly understanding, that a man can become, little by little, entangled in a life he has not deliberately sought and from which he can extricate himself only with the greatest difficulty.

13

S OME of the depression engendered by the discussion with Prior William remained in me even when Grocyn and I boarded the stage that would take us to Reardon whence, Grocyn had been assured, Master Colt himself would meet us with a carriage to convey us the remaining distance to his home. Neither Grocyn's moderate grumbling at the anticipated discomfort of our ride nor interest in three merchants who were our fellow passengers distracted me sufficiently. Only when the stage had carried us some distance into the country and I began to notice the wild flowers scattered in the areas between plowed fields and pastures did I forget completely my own troubles. I realized that this was the first occasion I had had to leave London—except to walk the short distance to the law schools, which were really within London with respect to their surroundings—since I had returned from Oxford. With that I remembered how much I had enjoyed and how I had regretted leaving the open areas and clean freshness of the country. I leaned back in the hard seat, watched the fields and houses and few people we passed, and began to enjoy the journey.

Master Colt was a big, genial man whose muscular body showed a man completely familiar with the operations of his fields by actual experience with them. I could not doubt that, when his employees struggled to perform some arduous task, Master Colt could assist with his strength as well as his knowledge. He easily lifted our luggage, which the driver had set down from the top of the stage, and swung it into a compartment in the rear of his own carriage. While he worked, he responded cheerfully and lightly to the comments of Grocyn and myself. He was a dark-haired man, and his face was browned by exposure to sun and wind. Yet, when I remarked about the wild flowers, he was able to name each of them. While we rode with him, he described the crops that would appear ultimately in the fields we passed, though only the smallest parts of green were visible above the earth, then described relative virtues of different types of cattle we saw, until I realized that farming was not a menial task of laborers as I, Londoner-born, had often conceived it to be, but a manner of life demanding its own specialized knowledge. I was somewhat amused to remember that I had entertained some fears about this visit to the country lest my host prove ignorant while, actually, I was delighting in his knowledge and conversation.

When we approached Master Colt's home, I remembered a second misgiving about this visit in that his family consisted of a wife and two daughters. I felt some dread of spending two weeks in the company of countrywomen. That dread was dispelled by sight of his home, for it was so large that I would have no difficulty withdrawing from the company of the others whenever I wished. I decided that I could always plead the necessity of devoting some attention to my work.

Newhall is best described as the ideal country home, but Master Colt refused to use the term because he refused to use his home only as a convenience during the summer months, returning to the city in the fall as most others.

"I am a countryman and a farmer by choice, Master More," he told me. "My wife and I love the country and want our daughters to love it. We travel into the city only when business demands. Newhall is our home, not our country home."

The last of my fears as to his wife and daughters vanished when we entered the home. Mistress Colt was a pleasant, bright-eyed, happy woman, who found immediate basis for friendship by mentioning names of Londoners I knew only because of my lectures at St. Lawrence but whom she seemed to know as guests at her home.

The two daughters she presented were talented and entirely agreeable in appearance. The younger, Miss Mary, attracted me immediately by her gaiety and vivaciousness of manner. The older, Miss Jane, attracted me as surely though less quickly by her quiet interest in her parents' guests. Of the two, I could not say which was the prettier. I felt somewhat awkward in their presence, which I attributed to the fact that I had lived the past eleven of my twenty-three years in a completely masculine environment. In the privacy of the room assigned to me, I admitted that I was already delighted with this family.

Food and the eating of it was an unimportant feature of meals at the Colts. The dinner that evening, and all meals thereafter, proved to be excuses for gathering about a table for a period of gay conversation and laughter into which I was drawn first by Mistress and Master Colt, then by Miss Mary, and, finally, by Miss Jane. I could not remember that dinner at my father's house had ever been an occasion of joy such as this though, in justice to him, I remembered that he had presided over a table surrounded by children and that his pompous monologues may have been necessary to maintain order.

Grocyn alone seemed not to enter into the gaiety of that occasion, though he was not displeased. He seemed to have lived so long in those groups where silence was imposed that he could not easily dismiss the habit; yet he seemed pleased that I enjoyed Miss Mary's complaints against my seriousness and Miss Jane's defense that I was interested in serious subjects her sister would not appreciate. When dinner ended, Grocyn went with Master Colt on some matter of interest to them, while I willingly went with Mistress Colt and her daughters to the garden, behind the house, which was their joy.

Not once during those two weeks was there a conversation approaching the gravity of the conversations to which I was devoted with Grocyn, with Father Paul and others in London. Not one memorable incident occurred during the period. Yet I begrudged the days as they passed, and the nights that interrupted my pleasure, and decided that the whole, rather than any part of it, was truly memorable. When it ended, I felt, not a depression such as I had on leaving London, but a heaviness of heart I had never before experienced. Master Colt's invitation for me to return whenever I could, an invitation echoed by Mistress Colt and their two daughters, increased my melancholy.

Grocyn and I were the only passengers in the stage from Reardon to London, probably because it was Sunday evening or because it was the late stage in which we traveled. I slumped down gloomily on the seat, looking without interest on the dark countryside and continuing to stare into the darkness, where nothing was visible but an occasional light glowing from the window of a house. Grocyn, not now grumbling at discomfort as he had on leaving London, talked cheerily for a time until my silence discouraged him.

At another time I would have marked the change in him, but I was too deeply engrossed in my own melancholy to interest myself in analysis of my companion.

For three weeks, I applied myself stubbornly to the routine of life at the Charterhouse. Furnivall's and the courts were closed; most of those I knew in London had left the city for the summer; nothing offered distraction from my chosen way of life other than the memory which would not diminish. The pressure within me demanded release. I dared not talk to Grocyn, who would know the reason for it. I studied the matter for some days to arrange my thoughts, then asked Father Paul to my room.

"Would you resent a question about your family life before you came here?" I asked tentatively.

Father Paul laughed. He seemed surprised but also pleased. "Not at all. I enjoy thinking of it myself."

"Did you have brothers and sisters?"

"Four brothers and three sisters. There were two other children who died when they were young."

"How old were you when you left home?"

"I was nineteen when I came here." Father Paul seemed to penetrate suddenly the reason for my questions. His expression became serious and sympathetic. "How old were you, Master More, when you left home?"

I had not anticipated that I would endure any questioning myself but, in fairness, I could not refuse to answer. "Twelve. I went first into the service of the Cardinal as a page. He entered me at Oxford. Then I was placed in the law schools. You know the rest."

As if he completely understood he nodded. "You did not live at home long enough to know what family life is like, is that it, Master More?" He paused a moment, but

I didn't offer to answer. "You have been troubled since you came back from Essex, Master More. Was that the first time you really had seen . . . No! Let me phrase it differently. Was the family you visited a very happy family?"

I nodded. There was no longer advantage in attempting to conceal my thoughts. I related the pleasure I had experienced with the Colts. When I finished, we were both silent for a time. I walked to the window and looked out sightlessly into space. I could feel him looking at me, measuring me.

"What are your intentions now, Master More?"

I shook my head helplessly. "What should I do?"

"Will you be able to forget this or at least put it from your mind until God gives you the grace to conquer its attractions?"

I didn't answer—a device that seemed sufficient answer to Father Paul.

"I will advise you, Master More," he announced.

I turned hopefully.

"I will advise you to return to your father; live there for a time while you compare life in the world with life at the Charterhouse."

"I can't do that."

Father Paul was puzzled. I remembered that I never had told him of the scene on my twenty-first birthday when I had parted from my father. I told him now—even confessing that my father had seemed prepared to disown me—and saw the disappointment with which he heard of that day.

"I wish that I or Prior William had known of that, Master More. We knew that something has been restraining and impeding you. That was the key. Had we known that, you might long ago have been accepted into the community . . . or advised to leave this life."

"But others have come here against the wishes of their parents."

"A great many," Father Paul agreed. "There is one difference, Master More, between you and the others. You permitted yourself to become angry with your father on the day you came here and never attempted to re-establish your proper relationship with him. The others were not themselves angry—whatever attitude their parents displayed—and have never ceased their efforts to restore the relationship that should exist between son and parents."

I saw that any further effort to defend myself would lead only to a blunt accusation of pride. At the moment, I admitted that perhaps the pride which Cardinal Morton had marked was still a part of me, but I wished to limit the admission to myself.

"Are you willing to visit your father and try to restore your relationship?"

"That would accomplish nothing except to make him angrier than ever," I answered.

"I asked only if you were willing to try."

I waited a moment and breathed deeply. "No," I said.

"Then you must have some other intention."

"I asked you what I should do."

"Would you be angry if I suggested that you visit Master Colt for another two weeks?"

I looked at him quickly. Within me I knew this was the suggestion I had hoped to hear. Father Paul began to smile as though he knew precisely what I wanted to hear and what he should say. He motioned that I should sit down, and he turned the chair around so that he could face me.

14

"WHICH is better, Master More: to be a learned layman of great holiness or a learned priest of little holiness?" I knew he did not require an answer.

"There is one great vocation for all of us," Father Paul continued. "And that vocation is the same for all of us. Our blessed Lord lived it for us that all of us would know what it is: to know the will of God as it pertains to each one of us and to fulfill that will." Father Paul's eyes lighted as he spoke. He seemed launched on a favorite subject. "How do we know His will as it applies to us individually? He will not come down from heaven to tell each of us what we should do. He will not even send an angel. He indicates His will and our individual vocations by implanting in each one of us tendencies toward different activities. He does not want all to be priests; neither does He want all to marry and be parents. He calls some to this religious life at the Charterhouse. He calls others to be secular priests. He calls more to marry. Men who try to force their way into the priesthood resist His will just as much as those who refuse a vocation to the priesthood."

I felt that I must defend myself against his implied accusation that I was endeavoring to force my way into the Charterhouse. "The tendencies in one may not be so clear as in another," I objected.

He shook his head slowly in disagreement. "God makes His signs abundantly clear, Master More. If we have difficulty discerning them, we should beware of our dullness of perception and not blame deficiency of God's light. I do not offend you?" he asked apologetically.

I moved my head without interest in his apology. His question was a challenge I could not refuse.

"A proud man will ask a direct sign from heaven before he will obey," Father Paul continued slowly and hesitantly as though alert to my reaction. "A humble man strives to discern whatever indications God provides, grateful that he is so directed."

If I did not understand the full significance of all that Father Paul said to me, I did understand that I should acknowledge a fault in my refusal to approach my father, and I should acknowledge the overpowering attraction to the Colts.

"I will ask Prior William to permit you to live in the guesthouse, as you have," Father Paul concluded, "until you are able to determine what your life should be. Use that time to reinforce your spiritual muscles."

When I saw Grocyn again, I said nothing to him of Father Paul's words to me. I was chagrined, however, to see from his expression when I told him of my intention of visiting the Colts that he attributed it to a motive different from the true motive. He faltered when I asked him to accompany me, then pleaded that he was unable to leave London for the time.

My second visit to the Colts was equally uneventful but even more enjoyable than the first. Life within that family was unceasingly joyous. In early September, I visited them for the third time and returned at the end of that same month with the explanation that, as the courts would resume in October, I would be unable to visit for an indefinite period. Consequently, I surprised myself and the Colts by discovering another opportunity for visiting them late in October.

By accident, at first, then by mutual but unspoken agreement, Miss Jane and I met each afternoon in the garden; thus my impression of earthly happiness is inseparably joined to a picture of flower-bordered paths circling in the small area between Master Colt's house and a grove of trees. An essential of that picture is a bench facing toward the garden, for this bench slowly elevated itself to the stature of a shrine where my tongue spoke the prosaic things of the world while my eyes feasted on the soft loveliness of brown hair and flower-petaled skin. Each appearance of the smile that touched her lips and lighted her eyes lifted my heart and hurled it far into space.

From the beginning, however, some barrier interposed between us. There were occasions when our conversation led us very close to it; then we would both become silent until one could devise some means of retreat. I wished to avoid it because I had no clear explanation for it. Avoidance had no magic power to dispel it, however, so it was inevitable that we must eventually set aside the restraint of formality to destroy the one barrier remaining between us. In October, I described a legal matter which I had concluded successfully just before my visit and was rewarded as usual by her smile and compliments. My whole being was infused with satisfaction.

"Master Thomas," she asked, "would you be offended if I asked why you engage in law and literature but live at the Charterhouse?"

"I went there to discover if I had a vocation for that life," I answered easily. "Father Paul, the Guestmaster, has helped to show me that my vocation is in the world."

She was puzzled. "Is that customary in London—to continue living there after you know you do not have a vocation?"

"Others have lived there," I answered. Miss Jane said nothing, and I knew she detected my evasion and would not inquire more deeply into a matter I considered secret. From that moment, I began to understand that the dispute with my father, which had interfered with my vocation to the Carthusians, now threatened to intrude into this new happiness I had found and which I could not bear to lose. She had no more knowledge than before of the nature of the barrier between us, but I knew that she was unwilling to ignore it. I knew, too, that to reveal the dispute with my father would be to endanger this happiness, for she would not be able to understand such a separation between father and child.

I was burdened with unhappiness when I returned to London, a burden so great that I could not endure it. I should have gone to court on the following morning, but my suffering would not permit me to give attention to my business there. My soul demanded relief from my pain, and I waited at the Charterhouse until Father Paul could hear me.

"The same problem," he remarked when he understood. "Your disagreement with your father is becoming more and more important, Master More."

I nodded, silently.

"You say that you love this Miss Jane Colt. Within what bounds?"

"There are no bounds!" I exclaimed.

He shook his head in disagreement. "The bounds may not be evident to you, but they are quite clear to anyone else."

I did not want to see those bounds clearly. "If someone would be an intermediary . . ." I said.

"Master More," Father Paul interrupted, "when we say that we love someone, we mean that we wish good to that one, whether the one be God or another human. When we say we love God, we mean that we will obey His commands—even His precepts—when our own desires would lead us to disobey them. When we say that we love another human being, we mean that we wish to do some good for them even though doing it requires sacrifice of some good for ourselves. Love means that we are willing to humble ourselves for another. If we are not willing to humble ourselves, the love we proclaim is but love for ourselves. We deceive the very one we pretend to love."

I had planned, when I suggested an intermediary, to enlist Grocyn if Father Paul refused me. His reference to deceit as an alternative to humility destroyed my plan. The thought of approaching my father flooded my imagination with unpleasantness; but deliberately to deceive Jane was inconceivable. However distasteful the task, I must myself end the disagreement with my father. With that purpose I went to the courts.

My father was talking with some others at the entrance of a courtroom. He did not turn as I approached, having learned from my conduct of those three years that I was accustomed to pass without speaking to him or in any way recognizing his presence. When I stopped beside him, he stiffened visibly as though expecting some unpleasant incident.

"I should like to speak to you privately," I said.

He glanced toward me, and I saw again some of the fear I had last seen when I parted from him to enter the Charter-house. I was dismayed by the thought that he might refuse to separate from the group and that my resolution would weaken before I had the opportunity to discuss the matter with him. Then he nodded excuses to the others and turned to accompany me a short distance from the group.

"I want to settle the difference between us," I announced.

The marks of fear disappeared slowly from his face and his customary smile returned to it. "I would have come to you long ago, son, if I had thought . . ."

Whether because of his astonishing words or the smile returning to his face, I realized that he had not changed. He was still the same proud parent he had been while I scored my victories at New Inn and at Lincoln's; and I had given him greater cause for pride by my increasing reputation as a celebrity in London. At once I knew that, had I come to him to mend our relations in order to become a Carthusian, he would have been as ready then as now. I felt a stab of regret that, had I been moved earlier to some small measure of humility toward that end, I might have achieved what was then the desire of my heart. Then intruded into my mind the picture of the garden, the flower-bordered walks, the bench, and the brightness of Jane's smile when I would tell her that the barrier between us was destroyed.

15

MY friends, the great of London, seized the announcement of my forthcoming marriage as an occasion
for a series of dinners and receptions, and for pressing on
me new matters to be presented in the courts. At Furnivall's
I felt a relaxing of the guarded attitude that had prevailed
since I began residence at the Charterhouse. Even a few of
the lawyers, of those I encountered in the courts, seemed
willing to forget the animosity generated by my identification with the clergy. Grocyn was delighted.

By contrast with the social activity in which I was
involved, our marriage was a quiet event in Jane's parish
church in Reardon. Of my London friends, only Grocyn
was present. Of my family, only my father attended; he
found favor immediately with Jane and her parents, as he
seemed to do with all he met.

When I brought my bride to London, and we made
our home beside the Guildhall, my friends inundated us
with invitations. They admired Jane and complimented
me without restraint. Elated with my marriage, elated with
my continuing success in the courts, elated with our social
activities, I assumed Jane shared my joy.

Just before Christmas of 1503, when we had been married almost three months, I was astonished to discover her
attempting to conceal from me evidences of crying. I had

seen children cry when denied something they wanted, and I had seen older women cry when bereaved by loss of those dear to them. Jane was neither the one nor the other, though the fact of her crying indicated to me a major cataclysm rather than the disappointments of childhood. Lacking experience in such matters, I made the mistake of exclaiming aloud my discovery of her and, thus, inducing a greater outburst.

"Mary is lonesome," I drew from her at length.

"Mary!" I felt exasperated that I had been led to so much sympathy and worry because her sister was lonesome. I remembered Mary's gaiety and vivaciousness, and the memory refused to admit the possibility that Mary could suffer in any way, especially from lonesomeness. "She is only lonesome because she has no one to tease and torment," I said.

"That is mean, Thomas More." Her tears flowed with renewed abundance. "I know she is lonesome, because I am lonesome for her."

"But you married me," I reminded her resentfully.

She raised her head to look at me in a bewildered way. Her eyes were made prettier by her tears, and she could have exacted whatever she wanted of me at that moment. "I didn't stop loving my sister and my mother and father when we married!" she said defiantly.

I tried to distract her. "Jane, you can't be lonesome. You had only Mary and your parents at Newhall. Here you have people around you on every side, you have hundreds of friends, you have your own home and a servant to manage." I waited expectantly for her to remember that she also had a husband.

"I love the country," she sobbed.

I jumped up from my chair and stamped dramatically around the room. "You have a husband successful beyond all others of his years. You have a husband who takes you into the best homes in London. How can you say you love the country?"

"I didn't expect to live always in the houses of your friends when we married." The remains of the tears made her anger more intense. "We are in their homes more than we are in our own!"

"If we do not visit them or accept their invitations, will you replace the legal business I will lose?" I challenged. "You knew I was a successful lawyer when you married me. You knew that I was successful because of these friends who send their legal matters to me. Must I give up those friends and their business?"

"Will children change your attitude?"

Whether the word or some delicate inflection startled me I did not know. Of a sudden, I was willing to surrender completely to her every whim, to abandon friends, business, success, the world itself—and I told her so. Her feminine intuition of a man's grandiose promises but reluctant performance protected her from believing my unrestrained words. Her tears suddenly disappeared before her laughter, while my protestations of repentance continued unabated.

"We will make an agreement, Thomas More."

"I will agree to your slightest wish," I said.

"We will go to Newhall for Christmas, and you will take me for other visits every three months," she said. "Every three months, that is, if I can travel there," she added quickly. "Then, whenever we are here, I will gladly entertain your friends and be entertained by them."

"I am the lawyer of this family," I protested. "The terminology of agreements is within my province." I made her laugh by hurrying to my desk, seizing writing materials, and speaking aloud as I wrote the agreement in sonorous legal terms. We were laughing and enjoying the delight of our reconciliation when Grocyn interrupted us—the first occasion in my life when I did not welcome his appearance.

"I cannot stay," Grocyn announced before either of us had invited him to remain. I noticed then that he was breathing heavily. "More!" he said despite the difficulty of breathing, "you are to receive new honors—the King has summoned a Parliament. A delegation is now on their way to invite you to a meeting at the Guildhall next week, where you will be nominated as a member. I hurried to warn you, but they must not see me here."

"Stay and meet them with me," I urged impulsively.

Grocyn regarded me disdainfully. "More, do you think they nominated you without some cause? I sponsored your nomination. If they see me here, they may withdraw it."

When I had closed the door on Grocyn, I swung back to face Jane. "Parliament!" I exclaimed. She smiled at me mockingly. I noticed that she was holding our newly made agreement in both hands as though prepared to destroy it.

"Next week is Christmas week, Thomas More."

A spasm of pain that was almost physical attacked me. I tried to smile but could not. "I shall tell them I have an engagement and cannot be present," I forced myself to say.

Jane jumped up quickly to fling both arms about me. "You said the words I wanted to hear, my Thomas More." She drew back from me without releasing me. "But your agreement provided that we would go to Newhall or remain here at the option of the principal. Is that correct?"

I nodded gloomily, still trying unsuccessfully to return her smile.

"Then the principal exercises her option of remaining in London during Christmas week and visiting Newhall for New Year's Day."

16

LONDONERS invented the name "Bridal Parliament" for the assembly summoned by King Henry for the beginning of the new year of 1504. We learned at Newhall that the country districts also adopted the name. There was but one matter of business to be discussed—a dowry for the marriage of Princess Margaret to King James of Scotland. The Parliament, therefore, was an honor to those selected for membership and an excuse for increased social activity in the city.

The beginning of that session seemed more a gala celebration than an assembly of Parliament. A great crowd of people filled the square in front of the Guildhall on the day of the first session, attracted by curiosity to see members enter the hall. So great was the crowd that they defeated their own purpose, for the members had to force their way through the press of people, and each was seen only by some small number who drew aside to form a path at the repeated cry of "Member! Member!" I had more difficulty than most because of my slightness and my evident youth, which led most to ignore my cry of "Member!" Only by great effort was I able to push through the crowd and gain admission to the Guildhall.

Inside the hall, in the large chamber of our deliberations, the same carnival spirit prevailed. Members gathered in groups, laughing and talking noisily. Men of the city shouted recognition of friends from country districts. The clerk pounded long and despairingly before establishing sufficient order to assign the members to their seats. As the youngest member, my seat was at the end of the hall farthest removed from the speaker's rostrum and in the topmost of the rows of seats that inclined sharply upward on both sides of the hall. Hardly turning my head, I could see all in the rows of seats descending from in front of me and all those in the seats rising on the opposite side.

Slowly and noisily, other members took their seats while they continued their conversations and called out to friends and acquaintances. The babble continued even when the speaker, Mr. Dudley, appeared at the rostrum, so that he was forced to continue pounding with the gavel as the clerk had done. At length, the chamber quieted sufficiently to permit him to begin reading from a long paper which, we knew, was the Dowry Bill.

The quiet of the house did not long continue. Mr. Dudley's monotonous tone and the interminable repetitions of "wherefores," "witnesseth," "aforesaid," and the like induced their inevitable boredom; the members began to resume their interrupted conversations. The speaker gradually raised his voice so as to be heard over the other voices—"for which purpose this Parliament hereby resolves to appropriate and tender to our gracious King Henry VII, the sum of £113,000 . . ."

Mr. Dudley's voice suddenly emerged clearly again as the rumble of voices stilled throughout the chamber. All trace of gaiety and lightness vanished. £113,000! I leaned tensely forward in my seat. £113,000! None had expected a request for a sum such as this. The house was quiet now, as though the speaker had just read the news of some great tragedy rather than a Dowry Bill. £113,000! When the speaker finished reading and took his seat, none moved in the hall; all seemed stricken and no longer capable of movement. I knew what held them. In the heart of every member was a dread of the popular reaction to the tax we must levy to accumulate such an enormous sum.

"Unless some member express opposition," the clerk's voice sounded the formal announcement, "the bill will be registered as having been read for the first time."

I remembered the last time a Parliament had passed an enormous tax levy; remembered the anger of the people that had been turned against the Cardinal. I remembered the statements I had made during the dispute at Lincoln's when I said the King was hiding behind the Cardinal's robes. That tax had been designed to raise the sum of £83,000. In an instant and without meditating on what I intended to accomplish, I stood before my seat and requested recognition of the speaker. He nodded toward me amiably.

"Mr. Speaker"—I saw some heads turn curiously— "seven years ago, this assembly appropriated the sum of £83,000 to enable King Henry to wage war against this same King James of Scotland." I was aware of members turning about quickly to look at me. "The sum was drawn from the people, Mr. Speaker, but that war never eventuated. May this House know the disposition of that money?" I heard some members gasp as though shocked by my question. I sat down quickly to escape the gazes of the members.

The speaker rapped his gavel sharply on the rostrum. "Your question is out of order, Mister More, because it does not pertain to the bill before this House." He gave an inflection to the word "Mister" in such manner as to emphasize my youth and make the House laugh derisively.

I jumped angrily to my feet. "I will rephrase my question, Mr. Speaker, that it will pertain to this bill. What assurance is given this House that Princess Margaret will, in fact, marry King James of Scotland?"

A sound that seemed a collective exclamation of dismay rose from the members. I remained on my feet. The anger aroused by the speaker's ridicule inflamed me, and I waited defiantly for an answer. "More!" someone called softly. "Withdraw your question." I would not look toward the voice and shook my head stubbornly. I watched the scene at the opposite end of the hall as several men gathered about the speaker. They counseled and consulted, looked toward me, returned to their conversation. Still standing, I enjoyed their confusion.

The speaker arose at length from his seat. "This House is recessed until tomorrow," he announced loudly and angrily. He rapped his gavel on the rostrum and walked from the hall.

Members surrounded me, some to beg apprehensively, others to demand authoritatively, that I withdraw the question. I pushed my way through them without answering. Outside the hall, most of the crowd of the morning had vanished. I was able to make my way without trouble around the building to my own home, where I might rest while my anger cooled. I could not disclose the cause of my anger to Jane; I seated myself at my desk as though attending to my work.

My anger ebbed slowly. I found satisfaction in having disrupted the speaker's apparent program. There would be no more attempts by him to ridicule a member because of youth. When morning came, I had completely recovered my poise and began to wonder, with some amusement, what escape the speaker would devise.

A noisy crowd was gathered again before the Guildhall, even larger than on the preceding day; but the aldermen of the city had provided uniformed men to maintain order and keep open passageways through the crowd. Someone in the crowd called "Master More!" as I approached, and I looked toward them but did not recognize any as acquaintances. Others repeated my name, and a roaring began in which I could hear them encouraging me to continue the opposition I had begun in the Parliament. This was, I realized, a popular ovation. Apparently some of the members had disclosed the incident of the previous day. As I hurried past, I could distinguish other cries to members following me that they should "support Master More!" The pleasantness of popularity remained with me until I was within the Guildhall itself and thought, for the first time, of the gravity of the situation that was developing. Once again, I remembered that tax of 1497 and the complaints of the people that had been turned by the lawyers against my patron, Cardinal Morton. Cardinal Morton was gone now, and the people could know that he had not instigated that tax.

The Chamber was quiet, noticeably somber when compared with the opening day. I went to my seat, watched others arrive and go to their places without speaking to their neighbors. I could see that London had been a place of industrious activity during the night and that the people had impressed these other members with their wishes. I remembered the cry, "Support Master More."

The speaker arrived, and some desultory exchanges began between him and the members. While my question remained unanswered no business could be introduced, but no one referred to my question. Even such a neophyte as myself could see that a game of parliamentary maneuvering had begun, prompted alike by the speaker and members, to avoid the matter before the House. Some members came to ask that I withdraw the question, but I shook my head stubbornly. I was enjoying myself. I had avenged the speaker's ridicule and embarrassed him. When the session was recessed again and I had gone from the hall, I was surrounded by a cheering crowd that ignored the restrictions of the uniformed men sent to maintain order.

Grocyn was waiting for me at my home. I could see by Jane's frightened expression that he had already talked to her. The anger that had died during the night returned suddenly at this invasion of my home and the distress of Jane.

I smiled reassuringly to Jane. "You needn't be anxious," I said. Deliberately I ignored Grocyn, put my cape on a hook, and went to my desk.

"You're playing the fool, More."

"You are in my home, Grocyn," I said without looking at him.

"And you are in Parliament as my nominee," he retorted. "You are disgracing me."

I forced a smile and turned around to face him. "Grocyn! What was it that you told me when you came to London?" I pretended to search my memory. "So long as you pleased His Highness, you would reside permanently in London. That was it! So long as you pleased His Highness."

"Thomas!" Jane pleaded.

"I could endure anything from Grocyn if he had not come here to frighten you while I was absent."

Noises in the street outside interrupted us. I looked out and saw that the crowd had come from the front of the Guildhall to walk past our home. Some in the front ranks saw my face at the window and began cheering. The entire crowd joined them, and I drew back quickly so that they could not see me as they continued past. I could no longer retreat. I gestured toward the window. "You wish to please the King, Grocyn. I want justice for the people."

"You're a fool, More," Grocyn repeated bitterly. He turned around to Jane. "I hope you can bring him to reason," he said, then left us.

Jane began crying again as soon as he had gone. My anger mounted as I tried to comfort her after Grocyn's departure. I had trusted Grocyn even more than a father. He had repaid my trust by his thoughtless effort to enlist Jane to his cause without considering, or even heedless of, her approaching motherhood. She quieted gradually as I repeated my assurances that even King Henry could not threaten a member of Parliament. "It is parliamentary immunity, dearest. Not even the King can harm a member either for his words in the House or his opposition." She did not regain her calm completely, but she managed at last to smile and to assure me that she was satisfied with whatever I thought to be right. The conviction grew in my mind that now I should not retreat but should hold tenaciously to my position to obtain justice for the people and vindication for the Cardinal. I resolved to expose this grasping King.

Through two more sessions, I sat silent while the parliamentary maneuvers continued. The crowds swelled larger and larger in front of the Guildhall to cheer me whenever I appeared and to cry out to the other members. At the next session, the speaker told a silent House that the bill then before the House was withdrawn, and he would read a new bill designed to replace it.

The House listened tensely as he read. I heard him repeat, word by word, the language of the bill just withdrawn. A doubt entered my mind once that he had merely withdrawn one bill and would supplant it with the same bill under a new title. "For which purpose the Parliament hereby resolves to appropriate and tender to our gracious King, Henry VII, the sum of £30,000," he read. A sigh of relief rose from the House. The speaker glanced up angrily from his paper, then resumed reading the bill in which none were longer interested. Members smiled and nodded to each other. Their voices began to rise again as the tension fled away.

I sat back in my chair. I could feel no exultation of victory. I was tired of the ordeal. The strain had been greater than I knew. Then I thought ahead to the moment when I could tell Jane of the victory won. I smiled, heedless of members who turned to look at me curiously. As soon as the speaker concluded and left the room, I hurried to the street.

A burst of cheering greeted me. The crowd had learned already, in the peculiar manner of crowds, of their victory against a grasping King. I tried to force my way through them, but now they would not separate and allow me to pass. I laughed good-naturedly with them and responded to their words. A great part of them surrounded me and escorted me noisily around the Guildhall to my home. There, at last, they allowed me to make a way through them and enter the house.

"Jane!" She was not in the outer room. I hurried to the

doorway of the inner room. "Jane!" My heart pounded. Jane was huddled on the bed, her shoulders rising and falling in great sobs. I rushed to her. "Jane!"

"Your father—"she sobbed. "The King has arrested your father!"

17

DARKNESS had fallen before I dared to leave Jane and make my way to the Tower. I stumbled often in the dark streets but could not slow my steps. I cherished a desperate hope that the arrest of my father was not related to the Dowry Bill, and the hope added urgency to my pace. At the gate of the darkened mass of the Tower, I hammered, then shouted, until a small shutter opened and a man's bearded face caught the light of a lantern.

"I have come for Mister John More."

The shadows on the man's face shifted about as he moved the lantern, apparently to consult a list. "Mister John More. Mister John More," he repeated. "Ah! Mister John More. Fined £100. Did you bring the fine?"

"£100!" I gasped. "I have not that much money." The man moved as though to close the shutter. "Wait!" I called. "What is the charge against him?"

The man looked down as though again consulting his list. He shook his head without interest. "No charge is stated."

I could hold no longer the hope that the arrest of my father was not related to me. The large size of the fine and lack of a stated charge were sufficient to indicate why he was arrested. The shutter grated closed. I turned away uncertainly.

I had friends nearby as I had friends in every section of the city. I rejected the thought as quickly as it occurred; I could not go about as a beggar asking alms of my friends. Some better plan must be devised. There were men who were close to the King and who could influence him. I plunged back into the streets that were like darkened tunnels and made my way, almost falling at times, to Grocyn's house.

His housekeeper opened the door and recognized me. From habit, she began to step back to admit me, then seemed to change her intention. "Master Grocyn is not here, Master More."

Her lie angered me, and I moved forward as though to push my way past her. "Tell Master Grocyn I must see him, Mistress Celie!"

She was frightened but yet did not move aside. "He cannot see you," she blurted.

The admission stunned me. I had thought he would not see me because of pique; now it was clear that I had spoken more accurately than I knew when I said he must please the King. Grocyn had abandoned me! He would not help me— would not dare the King's displeasure by helping. Neither would others dependent, as was he, on the generosity of the King.

I thought again of my friends, the great of London. I must indeed become a beggar. I could not begin immediately. Perhaps Grocyn's rebuff destroyed the courage I needed. Perhaps I was anxious about Jane, as I convinced myself at the moment. I returned home. Jane was already in bed and did not move. I hoped she was sleeping.

My friends had not abandoned me, I discovered the next day. None could offer extraordinary assistance; but I obtained ten shillings from some, a pound from others, two pounds from a very few. When I returned home that evening, I had gathered a total of more than forty-six pounds. Then Jane plunged me into new dejection by bursting into tears at my humiliation. I had no choice. On me was imposed the burden of obtaining the fine. I resumed, next morning, the pleas to my friends and collected another thirty-seven pounds. Having then exhausted the possibilities among them, I went, next day, to the courts to solicit help from my father's friends. There I learned that those who had helped with their money had told of my begging; the lawyers, who had never been my friends as I had never been theirs, enjoyed their opportunity to humiliate me even as they contributed to my father's release.

The taunts I endured made me reluctant to face my father at the Tower; but the injuries being inflicted on me became their own balm and sweetness. I was a martyr to justice, a champion of the people against the King, a man misunderstood by other men; my pride was comforted by the very multitude of insults. If my father wished to add to my troubles and burdens, I would endure all patiently.

My father's smile was somewhat lessened when we met in the room of the constable of the tower, where I paid over the amount of the fine; but he seemed to have borne his imprisonment without undue suffering. Neither of us spoke at the moment; I had determined that I would not answer whatever accusations he made against me, so I turned and led the way to the outside world.

"I am grateful to you, Thomas, for my release," was my father's first statement when we had walked away from the Tower gate.

I waited for the inevitable recriminations. We walked together along the street crowded with carts, merchandise, and people wrangling with merchants, who conducted their businesses in that outdoor market.

"Did you borrow any of that money, son?"

"I begged it of our friends," I answered shortly.

"Then it is a gift." He seemed tremendously relieved.

The enormity of his thought grew as I considered the relief in his voice and the words "a gift." He had not said that he would have been obligated to repay me if I had paid the fine with my own money; but I inferred that he would have regarded as a debt to me what he accepted gratefully from his friends as a gift. I was humiliated again; but this humiliation was unlike the others in that this was a true humiliation. He was my father; yet his measure of me was such that he considered it at least doubtful or even incredible that I would have been as generous to him as were his friends.

That this man, to whom I owed my very existence, esteemed me so little was a hard blow. Was it retribution? Had I esteemed him so little for his lack of talents, lack of learning, lack of those intellectual gifts in which I excelled, that he esteemed me very little for my lack of those qualities in which he excelled—his friendliness, civility, and politeness? I forgot my sense of grievance and injury, induced by the injuries to which I had been subjected, and felt a real disappointment that I was yet so short of perfection.

I mark that day as the first on which God granted me to doubt myself, my accomplishments, and my vaunted superiority. At the time, I marked it only as the day on which I first glimpsed some deficiencies and turned my attention from them quickly as I might turn my eyes from ugliness. Before leaving my father at his house on Milk Street, I had safely hidden the unpleasant sight of my imperfections in a dark recess of my mind where they could not disturb me.

Other problems distracted me. Each visit to the law courts inspired the lawyers I encountered to new thrusts and mocking laughs. I was able to ignore them and disdain replying. Then in rapid succession, judges of the King's court ruled against me in four cases, resorting to tortured interpretations of law to justify their decisions. A fierce anger rose within me against these men who perverted justice, and an even fiercer anger against the king who had ordered their perversion. Within a few weeks, I became aware that clients were no longer entrusting their cases to me, unwilling to prejudice their claims.

The common people of London did not forget me. Wherever I walked in the city, the common people greeted me, and their attitude served to sustain me for a time while my income and my spirits declined. I was able to conceal my fears from Jane, but the abrupt cessation of invitations and of visitors revealed our status to her. Her fears of the city and her loneliness for the country returned. She did not cry—or else concealed her tears from me—but I saw her depressed and burdened expression, and my worries increased. I began to welcome each night, when I could hide from all others within my home; I resented the necessity each morning of reentering the world and the affairs of men.

My father began to visit us. He did not speak of our troubles nor of any serious matter; he was interested principally in entertaining Jane, and did relieve her of much of her sadness. He seemed to understand that he could not relieve my burden of suffering, made heavier with resentment against the vengeful king and resentment against the friends who had deserted me in my hour of need. Yet his very presence benefited me also in a manner I could not then appreciate. He had not spoken unkindly to me because of the trouble I had caused him; in his presence, I could not speak unkindly of others, despite the angry, venomous words that welled up within me.

My soul cried for the relief of sympathy, and I could expect none from those with whom my mental and social talents identified me. In that time of need, when others had cast me aside, I thought of the priest I myself had once cast aside, then deigned worthy of slight attention when I had become a celebrity. I could not bluntly ask sympathy of Colet nor beg his understanding. I had first to determine his attitude toward me.

As I had before, I wrote carefully, concealing my true purpose, hopeful that he would not discern my intent as easily as he had when he was in Rome. Deliberately, I included a kind reference to Grocyn, willfully encouraging myself to believe that our estrangement was temporary and that we should, before long, resume our relationship.

A week was the minimum time in which he could receive my letter and answer it. The week expired on a Friday, and I anticipated receiving a message from that day forward. On Sunday, when I could receive no message through customary channels, I was astounded when Colet visited us, bringing Erasmus with him. As before, Colet had penetrated beyond the words of my letter and, not satisfied to write, had journeyed all the distance from Oxford.

Father Colet had changed much in the twelve years since I had last seen him at Oxford. There was even greater strength and manliness in his appearance; his smile was more subdued but expressed the same friendliness as before. Erasmus had changed not at all during the six years that had passed since he visited me. The two dissimilar men accentuated each other's individuality by their presence together. Neither of them referred to my difficulties but held their remarks firmly to the subject dear to all three of us—literature. Jane understood little the flowing Latin of our conversation but understood sufficiently that Colet's cheerfulness cheered her, and the sparkling wit of Erasmus made her laugh as she had not laughed for weeks.

They inspired me, filled me with an expansive optimism for the future. In the few hours, they turned my attention entirely to the life I had once prized but had forgotten, to pursue the fantasy of success and money and fame. Before they left, I determined to return to the first goal I had ever held in life. When they left, I was buoyant and hopeful. "Our troubles are ended," I boasted to Jane.

Her cheerfulness welcomed my extravagant claims. She laughed expectantly.

"Jane! Jane! I will do what I always could do. I will write. That is what I was supposed to do in life. I was not intended to be a lawyer. I am a writer and never should have done anything else."

"You will be a great writer, Thomas More," Jane added, and our spirits soared.

"The very greatest!" I exclaimed. "Oh, Jane! I will make you proud of me instead . . ." Her glance warned me not to continue. I laughed. "I will make our family proud of me," I exulted, and she laughed with me. "But I will begin modestly with a translation—I will translate Lucian."

18

WE began together the adventure of a new life the next morning. I wrote energetically; Jane's confidence was a part of my energy, while the energy of my writing was a part of her confidence. Each day, I discharged what remaining duties called me to the courts, then hurried home to my desk. Neither of us doubted. So confident were we that even loss of my position at Furnivall's did no more than startle us and make us reduce our expenses to offset this new reverse. Arrival of the baby in the early summer added a new joy, greater than our expectations, for now our love was embodied tangibly. When I recovered sufficient calm, I returned with greater enthusiasm to my desk, more eager than before; I had the confidence of both Jane and baby Margaret to sustain me.

I wrote steadily through the remainder of that year. As my law business and income continued to decline, I had more time for the work at my desk. Early in 1505, the work was finished, and I held the papers proudly before Jane and Margaret. The baby smiled unknowingly but without restraint. Jane smiled proudly but weakly; the burden of caring for Margaret while giving strength to our second child depleted her energy. I hurried to the printers with the precious manuscript. Having delivered it and expressed myself volubly as to the quality of work expected, I began immediately a history of King Richard III.

I had now three principal interests. I had still some cases to attend at court. I had the matter of the manuscript at the printers, whom I visited often to inspect progress of the work. I had the new and incomparably more interesting task of recreating the tyrannical and murderous King Richard. Burdened with these, I resented the distraction caused by Margaret's early efforts to walk, since those efforts were applied in the same room where I endeavored to concentrate my attention at my desk. I suffered silently for the time, anticipating relief after the birth of our second child. When Elizabeth was born and Jane was able once more to give attention to household matters, I found it necessary to complain that Margaret was permitted to intrude and interrupt my work. "I can't divide my attention between the child and my work. I must work either as writer or nursemaid; I cannot do both."

Jane seemed not to understand the seriousness of my complaint. I was forced to explain at greater length the importance of my work, but my explanation seemed to distress her.

"You can't put all else aside in favor of your work," she objected.

I waved both arms above the papers before me. "I can't apply my mind to this and to Margaret also," I protested.

My attitude seemed to hurt Jane but, rather than admit a new distraction, I ignored her manner and applied myself to my work. From that time, I was relieved of the presence of the child whenever I worked at the desk. Jane, too, entered the room as infrequently as possible. There would be sufficient time in the future, I assured myself, after I had established myself in my new career.

The translation of Lucian issued from the printer a month after the birth of our second baby, Elizabeth.

I feasted my eyes proudly on the finished work, letting them linger on the notice "by Thomas More," and carried a copy triumphantly home to Jane.

"It's finished, Jane," I called loudly as soon as I entered.

From the inner room, Jane answered softly. I could not understand her words, but I knew she was asking silence that the children would sleep. I walked into the room impatiently, where Jane was holding the baby in her arms while she rocked Margaret's cradle. Silently I held the completed work before her eyes. She looked at it absently, then nodded her head toward the outer room.

I did not wait in the outer room as she had indicated. I hardly paused there. I had to expel by physical action my resentment at her lack of interest in this matter so important to both of us. I snatched up my hat and went out to wander through the streets. People and the noises of the city intensified rather than relieved my anger; but I remained away from my home sufficiently long so that Jane would realize what an injury she had inflicted on me.

When I returned, Jane was sitting disconsolately on the long bench at the side of the room opposite to my desk. I had succeeded in my purpose of expressing my resentment, but now her tears vitiated my achievement. I sat down uncomfortably beside her, unwilling to recognize my fault and, therefore, unable to offer comfort. She bridged the inestimable distance between us by leaning toward me and resting her head against me so that I could not refuse to put my arm around her and draw her closer.

"Why must you be so proud, Thomas?"

So softly and miserably did she ask that she seemed almost to accuse herself instead of me. In her mind, we were one indeed, to such extent that the actions of either were those of both. I could only wonder myself at the terrible force within me that drove me to hurt the very one I held most dear.

"We can't put the children aside—put them into a closet until we are willing to bring them out," she whispered. "Oh, Thomas, no work is more important than they are."

"We must have food," I offered.

"God will provide the food—and whatever else we need if we only attend to our duties."

"My duty is to write."

She shook her head against my chest. "Your duty is only to support your family, however you can, but to love them also."

To plead or argue would be futile. I offered no more objections. We had resolved our differences, and that was satisfying in itself. When I was established in my new career, we would be able to arrange matters so that my family and my work would not conflict.

Almost from the beginning, I saw—and ignored—evidence that my first book was a failure. Day after day I went eagerly to the printers to obtain a report of sales. Early reports were discouraging, and I went less frequently. In August—it was the year 1506—I accepted at last the realization of my failure.

"Lucian has failed," I told Jane.

She nodded. I expected another outburst of tears, but she was more concerned with my disappointment than her own, as if she had known even before my announcement. Either intuition or the steady decline of my buoyancy had informed her before I was willing to accept the evidence that the career, begun so hopefully, had ended. Without quite knowing the reason, I kissed her and sought relief again by wandering through the streets.

Whether the streets were crowded or empty, I did not know. Neither was I aware of the places I passed or the turnings. A heavy weight burdened me and numbed me to the world outside myself. I heard again the taunts of those who had laughed at my defeat by King Henry; my heart writhed with disappointment that I had not achieved the victory that would have negated their taunts. I heard my own hopeful voice exulting to Jane, "I am a writer . . . the very greatest . . . was never intended to be a lawyer . . . never should have attempted to do anything else." My voice mocked me. The enormity of my failure grew before me. I had failed not only myself; I had failed Jane, had failed Margaret, had failed Elizabeth. I had failed even my father, who had long ago objected to my ambitions but who had respected my efforts by his silence during his visits while I worked at the desk. This was the second time that I had been proved wrong in opposition to him. I had acknowledged, by leaving the Charterhouse, that I had not the vocation I had claimed. I had now to acknowledge that I should have "imitated my betters without striving to equal them."

Night had come when I became conscious of my surroundings. I was standing on the bridge—the bridge over which my father had taken me to begin life as a page of the Archbishop. It was a life that had started with the greatest promise—promise so great that His Grace had befriended me and sent me to Oxford—but a life that I had forced into many strange ways.

The water flowed below me, forming heavy swirls where it touched against the stone supports of the bridge. There was little light from the few lanterns along the bridge. Where the light touched, the water was less dark than the surface farther away. I let myself watch, looking into the abyss of darkness. There was this manner of avoiding the admission of my mistakes.

I remembered His Grace's words of so long ago, "Your son has talents which can destroy him if his pride is not curbed"; and Colet's letter that I had not sufficient humility to live the Carthusian life. From the darkness below me I heard Jane's voice questioning again. "Why must you be so proud, Thomas?" I groaned to the water below me.

The sound of my own voice distracted me from the darkness before me. The light of hope flickered faintly as a candle just before it expires, terrorizing me with the concept of what I was about to do. But in that moment of flickering, I turned away and ran as quickly as I could, heedless of obstacles that might lie in my path. The terrible vision strengthened my body as I ran desperately from the bridge.

In my own house, I had not to call; Jane cried out to me even as I opened the door, then clung to me desperately as though she knew all the dread ordeal. It was I who cried and she who comforted. "We must go away," I told her—"away from London." I felt her head bobbing in quick agreement.

"Wherever you wish," she said calming me.

19

JANE would not agree at once, but I prevailed at last that she and the children should visit Newhall while I journeyed elsewhere. I could not remain with them; I could not endure to live before the eyes of those whose daughter and grandchildren I had failed. When I had delivered them safely to the haven of Newhall, I went to relatives of my own in Coventry.

Others rode as passengers in the stage from Reardon, but I had no interest in them. I had a feeling of safety merely in the knowledge that I was progressing farther from London and the dread bridge. Without volition, my mind turned back to that night, to the groan that had aroused me. Had I actually groaned? Whether I had was not important. That I had run from that temptation was all-important—that I continue to run was equally important. If I were so weak that only flight had saved me from that night, how weak might I be in some other temptation?

I felt the passenger beside me—a man—watching me curiously. Perhaps I had made some sound, perhaps I had groaned again. I tried to divert my mind and hold attention to the countryside that once had delighted me.

The immensity of God's awful power and justice engulfed me. I had deluded myself that I was virtuous and holy. What excuse would I offer God for my pride—that pride seen so clearly by Archbishop Morton, by my father, by Colet, by Jane—that pride to which I had been completely blind? What, other than pride, had deluded me with thoughts of a vocation, what else had led me to oppose the advice of Colet, to resent the interference of my father, to assert my superiority over my fellows in law school, to luxuriate in the compliments to my holiness while I resided at the Charterhouse? What, other than pride, had led me to oppose King Henry, who had so often demonstrated his power and vengefulness? What, other than pride, had led me to the very brink of destruction? An indescribable fear of God possessed me.

In Coventry I forgot that the purpose of my visit was to distract myself; I sought to unburden my soul in confession, accusing myself of sin in every thought and every action that had contributed to the moment of terror on the bridge. The priest seemed unable to understand the gravity of my offenses. I saw my life as a continuous series of sins that God would raise against me—an incessant pride that would bar me from the eternal happiness of heaven. Twice again I returned to the same priest during the week I remained in Coventry; each time I was more dissatisfied than before, more certain of eternal damnation. I could not quiet my fears with the thought of God's mercy; I was enthralled by the concept of His immutable justice. When the week ended, I mounted the stage for the return to Reardon, hopeful that reunion with Jane and the children would dissipate my fears.

That hope reminded me that Jane, also, was depressed by our common trouble. If she had been more cheerful than I, she was yet burdened with fear for the future. I felt some relief, then, to return to a wife who revealed no indication of past trouble or future worry. Jane came to Reardon in the carriage with her father to carry me to Newhall. She was smiling as I remembered she always had smiled before we married.

"I've met the most wonderful couple," she confided. "Tell Thomas about them, Father."

Master Colt laughed at Jane's enthusiasm. "Your wife doesn't flatter her parents, Master More. For two days she would hardly speak to any at home. Then, the Middletons came. Mistress Alice took her off to her room that very afternoon, and she has been as happy as this"—he nodded toward Jane—"ever since."

"They are our neighbors in London, Thomas," Jane added. "They live directly opposite our house on the other side of the Guildhall."

I was curious but little interested in the unknown Alice Middleton who had so quickly restored Jane. The fact that Jane had recovered relieved me of worry about her and thus opened my mind to the return of my own fears. I tried to appear relieved and happy with the knowledge of Jane's good spirits; but my very soul was burdened with anxiety. I wanted desperately to return to London to consult Father Paul.

When I was presented to the Middletons, on arrival at Newhall, I met a Mistress Alice who was not at all the soft, sympathetic woman I had expected. I had the distinct feeling that Mistress Alice probed my very depths in the moment of introduction. She was a straight-figured, slender woman, some seven years older than I, quick and precise of movement. Her eyes were coldly appraising, though this impression was countered by some gentleness of mouth. Master Middleton was a tall, quiet, and pleasant man, much like Jane's father.

Mistress Alice bobbed her head when we met. "Everyone in London knows the name of Master More," she acknowledged. I did not know whether she referred to the Thomas More who had lectured at St. Lawrence or the More who had been publicly humiliated by the King. Whichever she meant, I resented her words as I resented the feeling that she read my inmost and secret fears. I wondered about this woman's effect on Jane. I wondered also when I saw her attraction for little Margaret. The child greeted me but returned almost immediately to the side of Mistress Alice.

I became better acquainted with the Middletons at dinner and during the evening. Master Middleton was one of the numerous small merchants of the city, and his interests concentrated on his business activities. Almost as soon as dinner began, he referred to my reputation as a lawyer and asked me a question about procedure in a legal matter. I answered without interest but with some effort to make my answer intelligible. The answer seemed to surprise him.

"I never thought—none of the others ever suggested such a course as that," he exclaimed.

I thought automatically of the stupidity characterizing the majority of lawyers in the city before remembering my more recent reflections on my pride. "There are several precedents," I assured him.

There was a brief period of silence marking the end of the exchange. Before others could introduce new matter of conversation, Mistress Alice spoke sharply, "Speak, Master Middleton. Speak!"

Master Middleton laughed good-naturedly at his wife's command. "I am not as quick as you, Alice." He turned again to me. "My wife demands that I ask you to handle this matter, Master More. Would you be willing?"

I did not welcome association in a case that might bring me closer to this man's wife; and remembering the experiences I had suffered in the courts since I had incurred the King's displeasure, I was about to decline. But thought of the fee intruded before I could refuse. Then I considered again the nature of Master Middleton's problem; it was such a case, I decided, that could be tried in the Sheriff's Court of London. Sheriffs and undersheriffs were dependent, not on the King, but on the people of the city whose friendship I had won by that same defiance that had incurred the hatred of the King. "I will call at your place of business as soon as you return to London," I said.

Jane and I returned with the children to our home the following day. Attending to the children and our luggage occupied my mind during the hours of travel but, when the quiet of night returned, my fears returned with greater intensity than before. Through long hours, I lay quietly while my mind turned and twisted, tortured by the imminence of death, certainty of judgment, fear of hell. Regularly, the great bell of St. Paul's sounded the hours of the night, granting some respite from my torments. With the last note, I returned again to my fears. At last I slept, but so fitfully and for such a short time that, when morning came, my fears multiplied because of my physical weariness. As soon as I could leave without arousing Jane's curiosity, I hurried to the Charterhouse. I was grimly determined to accuse myself systematically and fully.

Father Paul shook his head disapprovingly when I told him my fears, my dissatisfaction with the priest at Coventry, and asked that he hear my confession.

"I have no greater power of absolution than the priest at Coventry," he objected.

"You will understand me and impose a fitting penance," I insisted.

"I cannot impose any greater penance than our blessed Saviour did."

His comment baffled me as he intended it should.

"You wish to protest to God your sinfulness; is that your purpose, Master More? Another man once did that directly to our Lord. Do you recall the words and actions of St. Peter? Our Lord had just given him a tremendous gift—a full boatload of fish—and Peter became so fearful that he begged our Lord to depart from him. Was that what we should expect of a rational man—that he would beg his benefactor to leave him? That was the action of a fearful man, a man who glimpsed the infinite power of God and who was so dumbfounded at the glimpse of His power that he could not contemplate His infinite mercy. Now, Master More, what penance did our blessed Lord impose on St. Peter?"

My mind was in a turmoil. I was disappointed that Father Paul was endeavoring to turn me away from my purpose; but I could answer his question. "Follow me!"

Father Paul nodded. "Follow me!" he repeated. "And leaving all things, Master More, they followed Him. That is the only solution—leaving all things."

"That was a different age, Father Paul," I reminded him. "Holy Mother Church would not countenance my leaving my wife and children."

"To God, all ages are one age. What He said to one age He said to all ages. Leaving all things does not mean a physical separation." He smiled slightly. "Surely you want to see your wife and children walk beside you on the way to heaven. Leaving all things means for you that you place

God's interests first, that you do something for God when you would much rather devote your time and efforts to some interest of your own."

"What?" I challenged.

Father Paul considered for a moment. "I would say, first, Master More, that God wants you to leave, for a time, your own judgment in spiritual matters and submit completely to whatever your confessor advises."

"I am responsible to God for my conscience," I protested.

"Conscience is the voice of reason, Master More. While you are subject to these terrible fears, your reason will not function properly, any more than did St. Peter's." He waited, but I did not speak. "You are a legal adviser, Master More. Many clients who come to you are fearful of some great loss. So your first requirement is that they entrust the matter entirely to you. I am a spiritual adviser, Master More, and must do as you would."

He forced from me a reluctant submission. At that instant, I was conscious of relief. My fears did not vanish, but they diminished because of his confidence, and I was encouraged for the future. "Pray!" Father Paul exhorted. "Pray incessantly for perseverance during this time of trial. Ask St. Peter to strengthen your faith as his own was strengthened when our Lord bade him, 'Follow me!'"

BOOK II

1

I WENT to Master Middleton, as I had promised, to begin work on the first law case assigned to me in more than a year. I was not happy at the prospect of applying myself strenuously again to the law; but I cherished a hope that perhaps some greater attention to legal business and less attention to writing was the sacrifice God asked of me.

The case entrusted to me by Master Middleton inaugurated a new era. I won judgment without difficulty and in such manner that the Sheriff himself complimented me from his high bench, thereby causing more discussion of the case than it deserved. Master Middleton was delighted and demanded that, thereafter, I represent all his interests before the court. Then, genial and grateful man that he was, he praised me so highly to his fellow merchants that he convinced them to assign their interests also to my care.

My fortune improved steadily with my newly regained fame. Cases flowed into my hands from Master Middleton and other merchants in increasing number. Most of them required presentation only in the Sheriff's Court, where I was invariably successful. Those cases that must be presented in the King's Court I delivered to lawyers reputed to enjoy the King's favor.

Jane was happier and more content than she had ever been in London; our new friends, the merchants whom

I represented in the court, seemed more agreeable to her as though more nearly like the people she had known in the country. The major cause of her happiness, however, was her friendship with Mistress Alice and the older woman's affection for her and the children. When Cecily, our third child, was born in January of 1508, Mistress Alice took Margaret and Elizabeth to her own home, relieving Jane of their care and me of an unwelcome responsibility.

Between Mistress Alice and myself there existed more respect than friendship. My respect for her increased during the weeks that she cared for the two children. She was not a stranger to them, but neither was she such a familiar as to explain their contentment and the manner in which she consoled their separation from Jane. I could discern few external indications of her affection for the children, but they seemed never to doubt it.

Even so, I was not happy. I disliked the law as much as ever I had. Multiplication of the number of cases referred to me evidenced my success in the eyes of others but meant to me only that I was becoming ever more entangled in an activity I disliked with increasing intensity. The improvement of my fortune, derived from law, was not and never could be sufficient to compensate for the lost pleasure of writing. I was forced so to reduce the time allotted to writing the history of King Richard III that I might as well have discontinued it altogether, so small was my progress. As weeks passed, my hope that greater attention to legal duties was the sacrifice God asked of me slowly evaporated; the fears that had taken root in me while I rode the stage from Reardon to Coventry continued. I was conscious, every moment of the day, of God's power, of His displeasure with a proud man, of my own pride so often demonstrated. My efforts to attend to law and ignore writing brought me no closer to that glimpse of God's mercy Father Paul had promised.

In June of that year, 1508, while the Middletons were visiting us, Jane told them our plans to visit Newhall during the summer and invited them to accompany us. Mistress Alice's shrewd eyes turned immediately and briefly on me, reviving the discomfort I had felt when I had first met her and from which I had never completely recovered. She made me conscious of the turmoil raging within me, a conflict I had hidden from Jane and wished to hide from all others.

"Master Thomas would do well to enjoy a vacation alone," she answered Jane. "With his legal business, his writing, and the children to disturb him, he should have time away from all three."

"He should," Jane agreed immediately, as I think she would have agreed to whatever Mistress Alice suggested. "You should have a vacation all your own, dear," she urged me.

I smiled casually to avoid agreement or disagreement. I knew that Mistress Alice was telling me I could not continue application to both law and writing. She was telling me that my ambitions to write were vain, that I should look objectively at the folly of continuing, should appreciate my talents as a lawyer, should be grateful for the life my family could enjoy because of my success at law. I must choose between the two. She was challenging me as both man and father.

I did not want to make that choice. I wanted to struggle longer with the law only to support my family; I wanted to write to sustain my spirits. I did not want to look objectively at the folly of pursuing two careers. If I knew, in my heart, the impossibility of continuing both, I did not want to perceive it with my mind. I wanted to delay decision, to continue major application to law only until God revealed His satisfaction with my sacrifice by relieving me of my fears. That relief would signal that I might again give greater attention to my writing.

Jane continued urging the course Mistress Alice proposed. I saw clearly that refusal would cause disappointment to her, that it would also cause loss of Mistress Alice's respect. I allowed Jane to persuade me, pretending to weigh the matter before agreeing while, within me, a new hope arose that a journey might distract me from my fears. At length, we agreed that I should accompany Jane and the children to Newhall but depart immediately for my own vacation on the Continent.

I went first to the university at Paris, to steep myself in that atmosphere of literature and learning and thus forget my fears. I found no relief there but persisted for three weeks before journeying to Louvain. As at Paris, neither the aura of learning nor strangeness of surroundings dissipated my dread. At the end of the second week, news arrived that London was seized by an epidemic of sickness that was devastating the city. I had found neither relief from my fears nor solution to the conflict between law and literature; to these was added worry about Jane and the children, and I slept only fitfully through the four days of traveling.

A London acquaintance, encountered as I debarked from the vessel at Dover, stilled my fears. Jane and the children were still well and safe at Newhall. Then he informed me that Master Middleton had been seized by the illness and succumbed. My relief at the safety of my family was countered by this information of Mistress Alice's grief.

I let one London stage depart, then another, without attempting to board them. I could do nothing of value for Mistress Alice, I assured myself, and would only endanger my own life by venturing into the city. I should guard my life and health for the sake of my own wife and children. I should board the small river boat that would discharge me on the shore of the river in Essex. At that point, I could board a stage to Reardon without once exposing myself to the danger in London.

I watched the boat prepare and leave. I could not ignore the claims of Mistress Alice; nor would Jane accept readily whatever explanation or excuse I offered for failure to help Mistress Alice. I must go directly to London.

London was a strangely silent city. The crowds had disappeared from the streets, seeking safety within their houses despite the stifling September heat. Funeral processions— a few acolytes preceding a shrouded form on a cart, with a priest following—seemed everywhere. I crowded into doorways to avoid contamination whenever I encountered these groups. The silence of my home where I deposited my luggage accentuated my cowardice. I hurried to the Middletons so that I would not surrender to the impulse to board the stage from the city.

Mistress Alice seemed to be two persons in one. She was the same shrewd woman I had always known; her eyes had lost none of their penetration. She was also a woman rendered helpless—a woman most unlike the purposeful woman I knew. Her expression lighted immediately when the servant quietly admitted me, and I was glad that I had not fled from the city.

"You should not have come to London, Master More," she said, lapsing again into her practical nature.

"I thought I might be of help," I offered.

She nodded. "You might convince my husband's chief clerk that he can release funds to me from the business without a court order." Her voice faltered when she referred to Master Middleton, but she forced it to regain a normal tone. Her lifetime habit of practicality was helping her to surmount her suffering.

"Master Middleton left no will?"

She shook her head briefly. She seemed about to say more, then decided against it.

"May I handle his affairs and yours, Mistress Alice?"

"Thank you, Master More. I am sorry you will have so much trouble."

It would be troublesome, I knew. Employees of Master Middleton's firm would delay proceedings in order to delay termination of their employment. Courts would delay. Other relatives might seek to claim shares of the estate. It was a sufficiently troublesome matter that I would not have offered my services except for my gratitude and, more especially, Jane's affection for her. Such matters were tedious, time-consuming, and unrewarding.

I did receive immediate compensation in the form of a letter from Jane, in which she extolled so much my courage and goodness in going to London that I was shamed by remembering the day of indecision at Dover. Something much greater, however, must have been granted me during the weeks and months that followed, some favor greater than the admiration of a loving wife, for the actual experience of attending matters pertaining to Master Middleton's estate was even more wearying than I had expected. Little legal talent was required for the work, but much attention to details. The monotonous regularity conflicted with my personal tendencies to avoid such uninteresting work.

The plague passed. Jane returned with the children and gave her attention to Mistress Alice as Mistress Alice had given to us. I forced myself to attend my self-appointed task. At times I looked longingly at my desk and the undisturbed papers of the history of King Richard III; but I had not sufficient strength remaining at the end of a day to resume writing. The months passed. Not until March of 1509 was I able to conclude the matter of Master Middleton's estate and give Mistress Alice the last of the papers.

I enjoyed that evening a sensation of freedom from the multiplicity of detail that had claimed my attention for such an extended period.

"You are enjoying the satisfaction of work well done," Jane said smiling.

I shook my head. "A clerk would have done that type of work as well as or even better than I. I can't force myself to like such monotonous work."

"But you did it," Jane insisted. "You weren't doing the work you like . . ."

I did not hear the remainder of her words. What she had said awoke both memory and consciousness— memory of Father Paul's words—"Leaving all things means that you do something for God when you would rather devote your time and efforts to some interest of your own"—and consciousness that I was free of much more than the details of Master Middleton's estate. I was free of my fears! The discovery burst within me. God had lifted that trial from my heart! Timidly and reluctantly as I had returned to London to help Mistress Alice, grudgingly as I had pursued the matter, God had accepted my efforts as though I had done all for Him—God had let me glimpse His infinite mercy to balance that glimpse of His immutable justice. And by that glimpse, my fears had been dispelled.

2

FREED of my fears, I was as a man freed from chains. That God had imposed those fears, I did not doubt; no other could have perceived the gigantic stature of my pride nor measured as accurately the weight required to crush it. Similarly, the relief pervading my whole being—heart, mind, soul, and body—was of God also; no other could imbue me with such lightness of spirit, energy of body, wit and quickness of mind. I exulted in the knowledge that I had suffered a great trial by God, had remained faithful to Him, and was now being rewarded by Him.

All things joined toward my well-being and happiness. King Henry VII, as though symbolizing the end of my travail, died in April of that year, 1509. None pretended grief at the death of the man who had ruled his realm with the same force with which he had won it. Some said that he had ruled well in that he had suppressed the nobles, whose warring with each other had held the whole country in turmoil for the thirty years preceding his reign; he brought peace to all England, they said. What they said may have been true; I admired the courage of any who were willing to speak good of the dead King to the people. Bishop Fisher, when he preached at the funeral, spoke but little of the King's life but emphasized that King Henry VII had been repentant at death—a more prudent and more beneficial observation than any pertaining to the King's acts during life.

England rejoiced—and I more than most others—that the eighth King Henry was, in all things, unlike his father. The seventh had been avaricious, autocratic, vengeful, and shrewd. The eighth was gracious, personable, athletic, genial, and learned. Our cup of joy filled and overflowed; we were as a nation inebriated. When the eighteen-year-old King Henry married Princess Catherine, widow of his own brother, the people of London celebrated through that day and all through the night. On the day of their coronation, the same people so filled the streets that the horsemen and the royal coach traversed a narrow aisle of cheering subjects.

Relieved of my fears and rejoicing in the accession of our new king and his queen, I poured out my own feelings in odes and sonnets, hailing the advent of our Golden Age. Erasmus hurried again to England from the Continent, summoned by a letter from one of his pupils, who wrote poetically and imaginatively, "The heavens laugh, the earth exults, all things are full of milk, of honey, of nectar! Avarice is expelled from the country. Liberality scatters wealth with a bounteous hand. Our king does not desire gold or gems or precious metals but virtue, glory, immortality." England—all England—rejoiced as though a long winter had passed and spring had returned to warm the land and the hearts of men.

My personal fortune increased more rapidly than before with the change of kings. The disfavor I had suffered from King Henry VII and his courts was past. All knew that an era of guile and craft was ended; an era of learning and generosity was beginning. The virtue of the new king was assurance that I and all others would enjoy fairness in his courts. Those who had been my friends, who had abandoned me, who had withheld their legal matters from me, now assigned their cases to me, such was the reputation I had gained by my work for the merchants in the Sheriff's Court. I accepted the work without enthusiasm; my business with the merchants was sufficiently prosperous, and the new era, combined with my new lightness of heart, promised that I might now achieve greater success as a writer.

Unrelated to other events of the day, but certainly a part of my own happiness and good fortune, was the birth of our fourth child and first son, John. Despite the recent bereavement she had suffered, Mistress Alice insisted that she care for the other children as she had before during Jane's confinement. Margaret and Elizabeth shrieked their joy when they learned they would live again, for a time, with her. The baby, Cecily, never once indicated unhappiness while in the care of Mistress Alice.

I discovered, about that time, an account in Latin of the life of John Picus, Earl of Mirandula, a great lord of Italy, and recognized it as a life worthy of both reading and imitation. I was attracted especially by the dispassionate appraisal of his pride and vainglory, of his proud appearance in Rome to defend 900 theses he had himself proposed, of his recognition of his tremendous pride, and his subsequent reformation. In these, I saw relation to my own vainglorious efforts, my proud lecturing in the Church of St. Lawrence, my arrogant attempt to pit my strength against the King's, the recognition of my gigantic pride, and my efforts to reform my life.

The most obvious difference between myself and Lord Picus was that God had blessed him with material wealth from birth, whereas He had entrusted it to me later in life.

This had resulted in a secondary difference in that Lord Picus had seen his responsibility in life to be the proper use of his wealth for learning and religion, while mine was to acquire some wealth for the benefit of my family. I put aside the history of King Richard III and devoted myself, first to intense study of this life, then to translating it as of greater value than the mere history of a tyrannical king.

Fortune continued its upward climb. In 1510, I became Undersheriff, a position that placed me beside the Sheriff as his adviser in the court where I had been markedly successful. More important to me was that I had gained power, not only to administer justice, but also to promote justice and charity between litigants who came before the court. Often, I was able to show either lawyers or their clients how to resolve differences with their adversaries without recourse to the court, encouraging forgiveness for injuries, mercy for offenses. I did not fear to encourage others to goodness and righteousness, for my reputation of virtue was established as firmly as my reputation as a lawyer, and none could accuse me of idle "preaching" rather than "doing." My regular attendance at Mass, at other devotions, careful observance of the requirements of God and His Church, were known by others. Joined to that original popularity, arising from my defiance of King Henry, I was as highly respected as I was successful.

I finished the translation of the life of Lord John Picus and was gratified by its moderate success and, more especially, by the compliments of my friends, who found additional reason in it for admiring my virtue. As though in compensation for those dread days when I was dismissed by Furnivall's, I received a request, rather than an offer, to become a reader at Lincoln's Inn. This I demurred in accepting; I was still reluctant to become more deeply involved in matters of the law. The success of Lord John Picus encouraged me to turn my attention again to the history of King Richard III.

The unvarying success of all that I attempted and the good fortune attending my family life was clear indication of God's satisfaction with me. I related the beginning of this era to my sacrifice for Mistress Alice in the time of her bereavement, and continuation of it with my regularity of life—of continued prayer and fasting, attendance at devotions, conscientious application to my legal duties. God was rewarding me for steadfastness during the years of trial and for whatever example I now offered when I had become a man of some substance. I anticipated that, so long as I remained faithful in every way to Him, He would continue His favor toward me.

While yet considering the advantages to be realized as reader at Lincoln's and comparing them with the pleasure to be derived from writing, the matter of decision was taken from me.

In January of 1511, Jane became ill. Initially, she complained only of small appetite and fatigue, conditions easily countered, the physician assured me, by the tonic he provided. Within a few weeks, her complaints increased. She was feverish and weak, and I summoned other doctors who assured me, as had the first, of Jane's ultimate recovery. I was not alarmed until Mistress Alice, who visited regularly, suggested that she take the children again to her own home. I did not want her to trouble herself with their care and told her that Jane would soon be fully recovered. She dismissed my objections.

Whether because of Mistress Alice's persistence or absence of the distraction afforded by the children, I was sensitive to Jane's decline. When next the priest came, I asked his opinion.

"That is the province of physicians, Master More," he answered and, in different words, repeated as often as I repeated the question.

A day later, Jane called me to sit close to the bed. "Some matters demand discussion, Thomas."

The forebodings I had ruthlessly suppressed joined together. I forced myself to smile at her. "Nothing is so important that it cannot wait until you are well."

She smiled weakly to tell me I could not deceive her. She caught my hand and drew me to the bench beside the bed. "You will have the care of four babies, Thomas More, and you must have instructions about them." I could not hide from her the spasm of sorrow, and she looked at me reprovingly. "I thought you were a man of God," she scolded lightly.

Her courage challenged mine. I suffered through the recital of her wishes and instructions without surrendering again to sorrow. Yet, when the doctors came, followed by Mistress Alice, and I was free to leave the room, I fled from the house to our parish church of St. Mary. There in a dark corner, concealed from all others, I released my sadness in tears. Then I remained to beg God's holy Mother that my wife be restored to me and to my children.

Gently and gradually, my courage returned, and I was comforted that, as God had blessed me with so many material things, so would He bless my plea that Jane would remain longer with me. I remembered His many favors to me and the blessings He had granted so abundantly. Deliberately, I comforted myself that He would grant this prayer.

When I returned to my home, Mistress Alice was waiting on the long bench of the outer room, holding a kerchief to her face. A great many people were hurrying about the room. Someone grasped my hand and spoke to me, but my attention had turned to the inner room, where some others were moving about. I wanted to rush into that inner room, but my strength failed me. I sank onto the chair at my desk.

A terrible temptation assailed me in that moment. I had returned comforted from the church of God's own Mother, only to be overwhelmed by this tragedy of loss. How meaningless were all of God's favors and blessings when He had taken from me that which I prized and treasured above all others.

3

MY father came beside me as I watched the first shovels of earth pushed into the grave. My mind turned away from him to grope backward again through the years with Jane. When next I was conscious of my surroundings, I was reentering the city, and he was beside me. I walked and turned as he directed, unmindful of streets, of people and all else of the external world. I did not resist until he led me into a building, when I realized it was the Church of St. Mary. I turned about to leave, but his hand touched my arm lightly, and I stopped.

Bitterness assailed me. In this very church, I had begged God's holy Mother to restore Jane to me and to our children. In this church, I had been comforted as though assured that my prayer was heard and granted. From this church I had gone home to learn that Jane had died. I stumbled dispiritedly into a pew and sat.

I knew why he had brought me. Often I had accompanied others to recite the prayer of submission and resignation when a loved one had been taken from them. The words could issue readily from my tongue and lips; I lacked the strength to speak them in my heart.

My father knelt. I, also, had done that when those I accompanied could not kneel. I, too, had knelt and prayed God's grace for my companion. I could see my father's lips moving. I knew, too, the prayers he said. What value was my knowledge of prayer if I prayed without love, without submission, without trust? When I had prayed for others, there had been no sorrow in my heart to impede, nor bitterness in my mind to distract. In those former days, I could protest, as blessed Peter, that I would die with Christ. In those days, I could even resolve, as I had that day at the Charterhouse, that I should be a saint. The reality of suffering destroyed the flimsy tissue of pretense.

Memory fixed on that first day at the Charterhouse. I would be a saint? Men would revere my memory? How pleasant the prospect! How easy the path before me! I had not counted the cost. I did not consider that sanctification of man is not the work of man but the work of God. I had not contemplated that God would work that sanctification only in those obedient to Him unto death—even to the death of the Cross. No thought of Christ's passion had disturbed my dreams. I would be a saint! How mockingly the words must have ascended before the throne of my crucified God.

My cross pressed heavily as I sat there. I could thrust it aside. I could obscure it by any of a hundred pleasures. Or I could bend forward submissively, lift my arms, as Christ did, to steady that cross, and begin the weary march to Calvary.

I had not the strength. I could not bear the burden. I could not submit. I slumped on the bench and looked vacantly at the altar. I had not even sufficient courage to ask for strength.

"Then pray only for courage!"

I stiffened, so clearly had I heard the words. They had been as loud and clear as though someone had spoken them. I glanced at my father beside me, but he had not noticed my movement. He knelt straight and motionless. Pray for courage? I had no desire to pray even for that.

"Then pray for the desire!" The voice was louder and clearer, more insistent than before; yet there was no sound. The voice was within me, urgent and compelling.

I could not pray. Sorrow—self-pity—numbed my mind and heart. I pushed myself forward and knelt beside my father. I could not pray. Let my action answer the insistent voice! Let the voice pray for me!

In what manner does God work within the soul, yet credit the work as merit to man? I offered no prayer—I had no prayer to offer. I could do no more than push my body mutely forward and kneel, more the token than the substance of prayer. Love impelled me, and God accepted that love, however poorly I expressed it.

Rebellion died as I knelt in that church. This world, created by God, belongs to God to be directed by Him as He will. This man, created by God, also belongs to God. The one must be subject to Him as completely as the other. I knew I need offer no other prayer. The slight movement of my body was sufficient. I had submitted. I had raised my arms, had steadied my cross, had taken the first step forward.

Self-pity had held me from instant and more willing submission. I had permitted my loss of Jane to obscure the right of my Creator. I had so cherished what seemed to be mine that I had failed to respect what was His. My failure and my fault were not born in this moment of suffering; they had taken root and begun their growth when, by the friendship of the Middletons, I returned to my legal business. They flourished and grew great during the three years past when my fortunes mounted so rapidly. They flowered when

I had been lulled to believe that all my fortune signaled God's pleasure and approval of me. I had cultivated that delusion of relating my fortune to His favor; I had no difficulty assuring myself a few days ago, in this very church, that Jane would be restored to me merely because I asked it. With prayers and fasting, I had demonstrated outwardly what my vanity countered inwardly. Prayer and fasting had become easier from habit; I had neglected the formation of inner habits of referring all good to the mercy and goodness of God. In a manner, I had halted spiritual progress, deceiving myself that I had not to strive as earnestly as before. I had been confident of the progress I had made and trusted myself to continue to progress in the future.

A hard core formed within me, replacing the softness of sentimentality. I saw my sorrow and suffering no longer as personal, individual, and barren, to be submerged and forgotten beneath an avalanche of pleasure or rebellion. I glimpsed indistinctly the significance of my suffering in the significance of Christ's suffering. Christ had submitted obediently to the suffering decreed by the Father—had hung for three agonized hours, nailed to a cross. My suffering, my submission partook of His suffering, His submission. In submission to the Father, I became one with the Son.

Self-pity died. My thoughts forged ahead with the current of strength pouring steadily into me. I could not serve two masters—our blessed Lord Himself had warned against the attempt. I could serve myself and my own desires, or I could serve God. I had beguiled myself that I had been serving Him, until the hollowness and counterfeit of my service was made evident to me by my reluctance to submit. True, I observed His commandments, I obeyed His Church; but I had not made His divine Presence the conscious goal and end of my life. I had allowed myself to be torn between my desire for writing, as my great purpose in life, and the necessity for attending to the law. My love for the one and hatred of the other had blinded me to the only proper goal.

No longer could I compromise, giving God only as much as He commanded. I did not serve my family nor even my clients in such beggarly manner as that. I had learned to expend my energies for my family. I had conscientiously discharged the duties entrusted to me by my clients and had done for them more than was required of me. I had given to God only what He commanded, grudging what He took from me.

I would compromise and deceive no longer. Loving and serving God would be the goal from this day forward. I would follow Christ, in submission to the Father, wherever the way might lead, however difficult the path, expending myself ruthlessly with His help.

My mind faltered. How would I know the way?

"Follow the path marked by your responsibilities," the voice returned instantly.

Responsibilities? Margaret, Elizabeth, Cecily, and John?

"Your father," the voice reminded.

The means?

"You were granted intelligence for discerning the means."

This reference to my intelligence seemed grotesque to me, who had used intelligence so poorly in the past. I would use it differently in the future; I would use it as God intended—to direct my actions toward Him. My father beside me had not needed great intelligence to guide him, but he was nearer to the goal than was I. Self-satisfied and contented as he was, his faults were blanketed beneath a great covering of charity. If I had greater gifts than had been given him, I had a greater responsibility.

The thought of his virtues recalled the purpose for which he had brought me into this church. I had no difficulty now; I recited without hesitation my prayer of resignation and submission.

I stood, and my father arose immediately, never questioning that our objective had been accomplished. He asked nothing of those moments when I had sat motionless in the pew nor of my action when I slid to my knees. He guided me along the street, as he had guided me from the cemetery, without speaking until we arrived at the door of my home.

"I can stay if you wish," he offered.

I shook my head, not to refuse him, but to assure him. "You need not be anxious now," I told him.

I wanted time to continue surveying the path before me, time to plan intelligently, time to foresee and appraise the obstacles. The memory of Jane would not distract; rather it would assist, for it was here that she herself had told me I should have the care of four young children.

A partial plan had already formed. I would accept the request of Lincoln's and become reader so that my babies would have greater comfort in life. That was the first and easiest step. The second would be to marry Mistress Alice so that my babies would have a mother. I wanted time to study and examine this second step.

That day and the next, I studied and considered. On the third day, I went to her home to visit the children but, more especially, to consider the second step of my plan in her presence.

The children greeted me noisily, but only Margaret was sufficiently old to continue interest in me. Elizabeth and

Cecily returned to the games that claimed them, John sought safety from me by retreating to the side of Mistress Alice. Margaret waited impatiently while I removed my coat.

"You did not bring Mother," she said in a tone that demanded an explanation.

I had not expected to be subjected to questioning; neither had I considered how to inform the child that she had no mother. I looked toward Mistress Alice, who turned her head briefly but emphatically from side to side.

"Mother could not come today," I told Margaret.

Mistress Alice anticipated the child's inevitable "Why?" and interrupted before she could utter it. "You are breaking your promise, Margaret."

Margaret examined me intently. "Are you sad?"

I saw Mistress Alice's signal. "Yes," I answered.

Margaret backed away from me, and I wondered at her action and the strange admonition of Mistress Alice.

"Master More, I told Margaret that you would be sad if she asked questions about Mistress Jane," she explained. Her voice was calm, but I detected the force that sustained the calmness. "You have a duty, Margaret," Mistress Alice continued.

The words diverted Margaret's attention from me. Her face lighted with a smile. "I am to care for the children while you and Mistress Alice talk," she confided. She emphasized "children" in such a way as to separate herself from that classification.

"I was afraid you would not be prepared for their questions," Mistress Alice explained when Margaret had shepherded her "children" into the inner room. "And I thought you might allow them some longer time before telling them of Mistress Jane."

"I was too busy thinking of their future to think of the present," I admitted.

Mistress Alice watched me intently. "What future have you considered, Master More?"

Her question forced me beyond the purpose for which I had come. Or had that purpose been achieved by observing her ability to anticipate the children's thoughts and the evidence of the children's affection for her? "I must marry again, Mistress Alice."

Her eyes hardened angrily. "You have only buried your wife, Master More," she said.

"I am not interested in a wife," I retorted. "I am interested in my children." I felt that the path was becoming difficult before I had well started. Living with this woman, however good mother to my children she would prove, would not ease my path, but I went ahead: "I came today to ask that you become my wife."

Mistress Alice looked at me wonderingly. It seemed impossible that this woman could lose her composure, but the blunt statement of my purpose amazed her. "You are mad!" she declared.

I could not resist the opportunity she offered. "I am inclined to agree with you," I said.

"I will not . . ." she began angrily. This once I was able to penetrate her thoughts as she was so accomplished in penetrating mine. I had told her my intention of marrying. If she refused my offer, she could continue the untroubled life she had led since the death of Master Middleton. But she would also lose the children to another. "Must I answer now?" she asked.

"I did not expect an immediate answer," I replied.

4

I KNEW what her answer must be. If prudence and propriety prevented immediate agreement, her affection for the children prevented refusal. So confident was I that I went from her home to my father to inform him of my action.

"A good woman," my father said, approvingly.

I went next to Father Paul. I anticipated that he would protest and endeavor to dissuade me from what he would consider a hasty and unconsidered action. I prepared myself to counter his arguments.

"You have not considered your position, Master More."

His objection surprised me. "My position is unimportant."

Father Paul's expression was grave. "Master More, Mistress Alice is not accustomed to entertain nor be entertained by the people who are your associates. She belongs entirely to the merchants. Your clients include all the great of the city."

"Clients!" I emphasized bitterly. "Not friends."

"What of the others?" he demanded. "What of Erasmus, the scholars of our own country and Europe? Master More, Mistress Alice has not the talent to be known to those people as your wife."

"I am no longer interested in learning, Father Paul. I am interested in the children God gave me. The children are my responsibilities; scholars and literature are not."

He accepted my insistence without further opposition. "I hope you do not think I object to Mistress Alice's character."

His question relieved me of uneasiness that he was actually attempting to impugn her character under the guise of objections to her talents. "I was beginning to suspect you," I answered so that we could both laugh.

He proved his good will by obtaining a dispensation so that the banns need not be read. As a result, Mistress Alice and I were able to marry quietly and without an audience, other than the officiating priest and the witnesses he provided. An unexpected benefit followed from this extreme restraint: The news of our marriage must have spread quickly through London, but no one presumed to ask questions or refer to it in any way, and I was spared the necessity of explanation.

I was not curious, nor did I care what opinions others formed. My mind was occupied with the next steps on the path I had determined on in the Church of St. Mary. I began the education of my three girls. It was an irritating and exasperating work made more difficult by Alice's unconcealed contempt for learning and the children's initial sluggishness. My patience evaporated one day, and the session with the children ended abruptly when I scolded Margaret, and all three children joined against me in tears.

Alice appeared quickly to lead the children away from me and quiet them in the seclusion of the inner room. I resented the obvious pleasure she derived from the opportunity the incident had given her. I resented, also, that she had exercised her right as stepmother against my rights as natural father. I tried to ignore this latter, unjust resentment by applying myself to the history of King Richard III.

My mind would not attend to the work, however, and I was alert to her return.

She ignored my apparent preoccupation at my desk. "Girls are born to be mothers, not masters," she announced sharply.

I swung around from my desk. "There are some who prefer to be masters," I retorted.

She waved her arm airily over my paper-littered desk. "What is all this gear—this learning? Will you be a kind father to your daughters, Master More, or a whipping-rod schoolteacher?"

If I had not yet attained complete humility, I had attained sufficient to be startled by her question. I felt guiltily that she, unlettered stepmother, was discharging her own responsibilities and endeavoring at the same time to counter my derelictions. I turned back to my desk without answering. I pretended to be absorbed in the work before me; but I was actually accusing myself. I found some pleasure in the realization that I was able to hear my faults without protesting.

The way pointed by my master plan of life was clear before me. If I was to follow the path of my responsibilities, I had no time for the pleasures of the pen. I was not being father to my children when I endeavored to force a calculated amount of learning into them within a specified time; I was merely being a writer who grudged the time allotted to parenthood.

Courage failed me. I could not give up the pleasure that was such an integral part of my life. For some days, I held myself away from the desk physically but had not the power to suppress the desire to return to it. Then I remembered the lesson I had learned in the Church of St. Mary. I began to pray, fervently and insistently, for the strength I needed to pursue the way of life demanded of me. Soon I received the courage necessary to gather up the manuscript from my desk and deliver it to the printer. I could not destroy it. I could only force myself to publish it despite my dissatisfaction with it and its unfinished condition. Once printed, it would no longer attract me from my responsibilities within the home nor distract me from responsibilities in the courts.

Having accomplished so much, I felt that evening that I was imitating the example of that great Lord of Italy, John Picus, who had destroyed his 900 theses, of which he was so proud, in order that he could no longer be proud of them. I felt the consolation of knowing that I was progressing on my destined way of life. I assured myself, also, that I had abandoned all ambitions to be a writer. Alice, too, seemed to exert herself to express her approval.

Henceforth, I determined, I would be a good father to my children—faithful to the responsibilities God had entrusted to me rather than solicitous of my own selfish desires. I remembered Father Paul's words: "When we say we love God, we mean that we will obey His commands and precepts even when our desires strive against them."

5

I FREED myself of that fatal attraction toward writing hardly in time to prevent complete destruction of the master plan of my life. Days later—on the Sunday following that eventful action—Erasmus visited.

"More, I am devastated," he complained immediately in his high-pitched voice. "I am alone. My dear Colet—my Plato—could not accompany me."

I felt, even while presenting him to my wife, that Alice was classifying Erasmus as an unwelcome guest. She saw at once his affected mannerisms, heard his high-pitched voice, then acknowledged him disdainfully. I was fearful, for the moment, that she would give verbal expression to her attitude, and remembered with relief that Erasmus understood few words of English and my wife understood as few of Latin. I explained the situation quickly to Erasmus, then to my wife, and told her that Erasmus would not be offended if she did not remain with us. I had chosen my words of explanation badly, for Alice turned away from us with such swirling of skirts and exaggerated daintiness of her steps as to ridicule Erasmus by imitating some of his mannerisms.

Erasmus seemed not to notice my wife's actions. He was looking wonderingly at the bare surface of my desk. "Your work, More? Your History of King Richard III?"

I smiled evasively. "It is at the printers."

"Wonderful! Wonderful, More! I had no thought you were so near conclusion!"

I hesitated briefly. I could not permit him to be misinformed; Erasmus would tell everyone he knew that another of my works would soon be published. "It is not finished," I confessed and pleaded my inability to be both lawyer and writer. I avoided telling him of my determined plan of life.

Erasmus was stricken that I would dismiss a literary effort in such ignoble fashion. "More! More!" he said. "The world stands desperately in need of literary men. It needs no more lawyers. What are lawyers other than troublemakers? They are never happier than when they discover a dispute that will earn them a filthy fee."

I laughed at his indignation. "You are speaking of me, Erasmus!"

"No, Thomas More! You are not a lawyer. You are a writer, a scholar, a man of learning, and a learned man. More, when did conditions in your country favor learning more than now? England's King is virtuous and learned—he surpasses all the kings of Christendom. He is a patron of learning and of scholars. He needs the talents of men like yourself, More—men who are known both as men of affairs and as scholars. Your King cannot continue to promote virtue and learning; he cannot continue to patronize scholars if other kings force him to turn his attention to wars. That is what is happening, More.

"Only one weapon can support such a man as King Henry VIII. Letters! Only men gifted with literary talent—men such as you, More—can turn the world against war and turmoil and strife. More, let other lawyers foment discord. Give your talents to the cause of learning and peace."

It was an impressive plea. I enjoyed the prospect his words built before my eyes: of defeating the sword with the pen; of countering the pallid excuses of warmakers with the vibrant truth; of promoting virtue and peace throughout Christendom. There was a time, a few short years, a few months, even a few days earlier, when the manuscript was still on my desk, that I would have considered no further but would have leaped into this role of world peacemaker. That time had ended on the day I had last visited the printer and divested myself of my literary career.

I shook my head slowly. "Erasmus, a man such as I does well—does excellently—if he succeeds in reforming only himself without attempting to reform the whole world or even one other person."

"You are the most virtuous of men, More!"

I began to smile, but his expression was serious, and I realized that he intended no flattery. The discovery amazed me. What measure did men use if they could regard me as virtuous?

"Erasmus, my dear friend," I said firmly, "I do not know whether I can adequately express my thought. Certainly there is not time to explain everything on which my thought is founded. But I think that a man's proper objective in life is to form himself or re-form himself into the image of his Maker—with the help of God's grace. God gives no man the power to persuade others unless others are willing to be persuaded. And even those so willing are more readily persuaded by example than by words."

"That is heresy," Erasmus exclaimed impatiently.

"You are distorting my thought."

"You are denying the efficacy of good works."

"On the contrary, I contend that all external good works

will flow naturally from this one internal good work that a man re-form himself. That is work," I said emphatically, "extremely difficult work."

"Good external works will inspire good internal works, More."

"I disagree. Eve instructed the ignorant, my friend, when she informed the serpent correctly about God's prohibition in the Garden. I can't agree that her external good work inspired any internal benefit."

We had never before disagreed on fundamental principles. Erasmus seemed anxious to discontinue the conversation before our disagreement increased. "I cannot understand you," he admitted.

I laughed softly. "I warned you that I did not know whether I could adequately express my thought," I said. I remembered my words about persuasion and knew the impossibility of persuading Erasmus. I was satisfied that I had strengthened my own convictions by the exchange and had acquired better understanding of them.

After Erasmus had departed, Alice and I deliberately avoided comment upon him. Remembering my own unfavorable opinion of him when we first met, I tried to sympathize with her attitude to the extent of avoiding whatever might provoke her.

Erasmus returned again each night of his visit to London, but on those nights was accompanied by Colet, and I hoped that Alice might be influenced to change her attitude toward Erasmus by Colet's evident admiration. On the third night, Alice had endured as much as her limited patience would allow.

"How much longer will he be here?" she demanded.

Her use of the pronoun instead of Erasmus' proper

name annoyed me. "Not as long as I should like."

She laughed. "You must be very poor of friends, Master More!"

"I became poor of friends when my friends abandoned me," I said sharply. "Erasmus and Colet befriended me at the very moment all others abandoned me."

She could not have been ignorant of the ignominy heaped upon me at the time I led opposition against the Dowry Bill. Her surprise revealed that she was ignorant that Erasmus was related to those days. But Alice was a woman who did not change lightly. "If only he were a man," she said sighing with mock regret, then disappeared quickly into the inner room.

The exchange with Erasmus on the day of his first visit, and the solidifying of my convictions, opened to me the next steps of the path I followed. It was then I began to understand that, as we struggle in the wake of Christ, each step reveals the next. It is a mountain we climb. If we attend principally to the matter of foothold and fingerhold immediately before us, we continue the upward struggle. If we turn our attention away to seek a resting place, our progress stops. If we look far above us at the obstacles between us and our goal, we become fainthearted; discouragement weighs on us and retards us.

I was progressing, but I was giving insufficient attention to my position of the moment and straining to look and to push higher. My position was becoming as precarious as a mountain climber who strains to climb the distance of a yard when he can climb safely only a few inches. I was so intent on action that I was becoming unmindful of the source of my strength—prayer and fasting. I had never discontinued the habit of fasting begun at the Charterhouse—a habit no longer difficult—but preoccupation with action had diminished attention to prayer. Having divested myself of literary ambition, I applied much of the time to prayer and some smaller part of it to my family.

My patience with the children increased measurably. The three girls—and Margaret, more than the others—responded quickly to the change. The time of learning became a time of joy to them and to me. Even little John, only beginning his lessons, engaged himself seriously with the matter of learning his letters and numbers.

Perhaps my diligence in prayer, perhaps some indistinguishable change wrought in me by prayer, perhaps the additional time devoted to my family, or perhaps my greater patience with the children was the cause—whatever it was, relations between myself and Alice improved noticeably.

My worldly affairs continued to improve as they had in the past. I looked to them no longer as a sign of God's approval; they were but God's gifts to be used as He intended. I did not exert myself to increase them nor did I hold greedily to them. My family had sufficient for their own health and comfort; if others needed, I did not refuse.

The manner of life I had planned, and which I followed in the four years following 1511, was neither interesting nor exciting. It was an apparently unrewarding form of existence—though some might judge it interesting because of the fortune that flowed toward me. My time was divided between my legal business, pleas for my clients, efforts to resolve differences and thereby avoid court proceedings, arbitration, my duties as Undersheriff, visiting my friends, instructing of my servants, and a great part with my family.

At times, this life I planned and followed weighed against my desires; weariness of the monotonous pursuit of virtue struggled to overcome the discipline I imposed on myself. The one compensation was the evident affection of my children, now growing to such age that they were enjoyable and promising of greater enjoyment; the one greatest evidence of progress was continued improvement of relations with Alice.

My life had been more interesting when I had driven recklessly and determinedly toward worldly achievement, even during the days of suffering when I had proclaimed myself to be destined for a career as a writer. When the memory of those days made the present uninviting and uninteresting, I returned more diligently to prayer to restore my vitality and move my reluctant steps forward.

6

IN the spring of 1515, conditions enabled King Henry to correct long-standing differences between our country and the Netherlands. Royal ambassadors resolved political difficulties, after which His Highness invited the merchants of London to propose a representative capable of advising his ambassadors about commercial matters so that they could conclude a treaty of commerce.

From the moment when I first learned of His Highness' invitation, I desired the post. I had visited the Continent only at that time when my fears had prevented enjoyment of the visit and the plague had caused me to return suddenly. I thought longingly of the opportunity this appointment would afford to live abroad for some time and to become informed of customs and people of other nations.

The post was, however, a great honor because it was a great responsibility, and I had become wary of seeking honors. I was sensitive that I could deceive myself that I wanted only the pleasure of the journey when I might actually be seeking the honor. Too, I was thirty-seven, somewhat young to serve as adviser to the King's ambassadors. So I restrained myself from such action as might have obtained the nomination.

At that very time, however, my name was discussed frequently. Only a short time before, my reputation with the merchants of the city and my popularity among the common people had caused me to be appointed Commissioner of Sewers. In that position, I was credited with certain improvements beneficial to the people. This, added to my long association with the merchants, and the reputation I had acquired in my capacity as Undersheriff, won the appointment for me to the King's embassy.

Once I was in Europe, my enjoyment did not long continue. Neither the ambassadors of my country nor those of the Netherlands desired a trade treaty of equal fairness and equal benefits to both countries. The two groups wrangled and accused, recounted past injustices, forecast future wickedness, defended their honor, and besmirched the honor of their adversaries until it seemed they were more interested in continuing indefinitely their positions as ambassadors than arriving quickly at agreement. In a last effort to exhaust our patience, or in retaliation for numerous delays caused by my compatriots, the men of the Netherlands pleaded that they must consult their King and must suspend the meetings for a period of three weeks.

The time specified was both too short to justify return to our homeland and too long to remain inactive in Bruges, the site of our meetings. We resorted to Amsterdam as a place of greater interest.

Long sessions and interminable disagreements had exhausted my interest in this embassy. I was mindful of my responsibility yet anxious to be relieved of it by conclusion of the treaty. In the leisure of Amsterdam, I became aware that some of my restlessness was born of loneliness. I wrote four long letters to my children and Mistress Alice in as many days. Four did not satisfy and, on a Sunday, I wrote a fifth.

The fact of my loneliness intrigued me. I had experienced no loneliness when I journeyed to Coventry and, later, to Paris and Louvain. I had not anticipated that, on this trip, I should regret separation from my family. I had welcomed the opportunity to visit this country of Netherlands; now I would welcome an immediate opportunity to return to the family I had blithely left.

There was but one cause, one explanation—the long sustained and monotonous efforts to be father and husband. Only ten years ago, Jane had accused me of pushing the children aside—even into a closet—that they would not interfere with my writing. Only five years ago, Alice had rescued the children from my impatience.

I had turned away from writing. I had become more patient. I? Had I done these? And had the doing of these incited my present loneliness? That had been the principle Erasmus expounded and which I had denied: that good external works induce good internal works.

I had not turned from writing, nor had I become patient. I could claim only that I had not resisted. I had not resisted when God moved me to submission in the Church of St. Mary. I had not resisted when He turned me from writing and turned me completely to my responsibilities. I had not resisted when He had granted me patience with the children and made me more agreeable to Alice. I could claim nothing more. God had wrought the change; God would continue His work in me as long as I remained sub-missive—as long as I moved, without resistance, along the path He directed.

Could I direct my life—could any man direct his life as well as God would do it for him? Yet men draw back, fearfully and timidly, from even the first tribulation God sends to call them to Himself. How ready we are to follow the leadership of men! Yet we flee from the sure leadership of God. We trust fortunes to lawyers, our bodies to doctors, our minds to teachers and scholars, our affections to others human as ourselves.

I sensed logic and value in the thoughts ranging through my mind. Idly I began to record them, without order, without knowledge of the end toward which I should use them. I had covered several papers before their import impressed me. I began to write more rapidly, hurrying to record each item. If men were made conscious of their dependence on other men, would it not make them more conscious of their dependence on God? If I were able, subtly and gently, to put that principle before men, would men—such as these men who had wrangled and fought over their conferences—turn their attention more intently toward God? Would they not use their intellects to discern God's will rather than to advance their own ambitions?

What would a world be that was peopled by men subject to God's laws as discerned by their intellects? Paradise? I rejected the word as inordinate. There was no need to picture Paradise. Something less would suffice, some lesser word that would yet convey dramatically the whole principle. Utopia! Nowhere! That was the word. Utopia—the world not yet known but which could be known if men lived according to the rules apparent to their intellects. I would tell of a Utopia where all men submitted willingly to law and responsibilities. I would tell the happiness possible to all.

During the two remaining weeks in Amsterdam, I wrote feverishly—seven additional letters to my family, and my vision of Utopia. When the weeks ended and our group returned to Bruges, I was rested from the ordeal of the previous conferences and resigned to their resumption. *Utopia*, a great bundle of manuscript, was in my luggage to be studied and corrected at leisure when I should return to England.

For a time after my return, leisure seemed as nonexistent as the land of Utopia. Business matters had accumulated to impressive heights while I was abroad. Legal matters of my clients demanded attention. Friends from whom I had been separated for the months of the embassy demanded a recounting of my observations of people and customs in the Netherlands. Thus, the year passed and a new year began before I had leisure to review and correct what I had written at Amsterdam.

I recognized at once that something more, some greater contrast with our world as we knew it, was necessary to make men understand the message I wished to convey. I wrote, quickly and confidently, another section, equal to that already written, saw that the whole was complete and unified, and delivered the finished work to the printer.

Much of my anxiety to finish the *Utopia* manuscript arose from fear that my old temptation was reviving. I thought to rid myself of it by hurrying completion of the book and turning my attention again to my family and my legal responsibilities.

The ease and speed with which I finished Utopia proved my undoing. Never before had I been able to write so fluently and purposefully. Previous efforts had always been hampered by external difficulties of money or family that had prevented me from giving full attention to the work on which I engaged. Those conditions no longer prevailed and I discovered that I had a notable talent, indeed, that produced page after page without difficulty and required little correction. I struggled against the mounting temptation to return to writing.

The *Utopia* proved astonishingly successful, hailed alike by scholars, nobles, merchants, and clergy. Men who had ignored my translation of Lucian, who had displayed slight interest in the *Life of John Picus*, who had complimented but not purchased the unfinished *Life of King Richard III*, found *Utopia* new and novel. So eagerly did they purchase my book that new issues were rushed from the printing press. Astonished and overwhelmed—one friend even termed me "the one genius of whom England can boast"—I could no longer resist the impulse of my heart. I permitted myself to consider other books, ideas for which were already crowding into my mind. I saw that my worldly situation was such that I could reduce my legal activities yet support my family while endeavoring once again to pursue the career of a writer.

Alice and I were inundated with invitations to receptions and dinners of the great, and I remembered, with something of a shudder, that time sixteen years earlier when I was the celebrated young lecturer at the Church of St. Lawrence and the popular young man among these same great of London. Alice, unburdened by such memories, displayed a delight in these social invitations that I would not have expected of her. An invitation to a reception at York House, residence of the Lord Chancellor, Cardinal Wolsey, astonished her and impressed her with the measure of success I had achieved as both author and lawyer.

"Commoners at the reception of His Eminence!" she repeated wonderingly. "Commoners at the reception of His Eminence!"

"The Cardinal is a commoner himself," I reminded her.

She resented the slight intimation that our invitation was not as great an honor as she wished to believe. "Wake yourself to your position, Master More!" she chided sharply. "Other men of this city would know how to make use of this to improve their fortune."

I did not attempt an answer. Her observation was accurate and unassailable. I could acquire a tremendous fortune at the law by turning my energies entirely toward it. I could even employ some number of assistants to prepare briefs over which I had always labored myself, or could use assistants to present minor cases in court, depending on the fame of my name to supply whatever talent those assistants lacked. In the past, I had regarded such devices as somewhat dishonest, but it would be easy to persuade myself now to a different view.

Deep within me was guilt—and I refused to grant it prominence—that I was no more certain of success as a writer than I had been before. True, I had written one successful book; but I had no assurance that others would equal its success. If others proved to be failures, my family would suffer some privation, and I could not hope that I might, at some later time, reestablish myself at law as I had before. I was thirty-eight years of age, an age not favorable to experimentation.

I felt that I had retrogressed to that earlier time when I had been uncertain of the future, and Alice had suggested that I vacation in Europe. She had perceived the struggle within me; she might see that it had returned. I doubted that she would be as sympathetic as before.

The possibility of retrogression from my goal accomplished what Alice's angry words could not. Deliberately

I weighed my desire and saw the guilt attached to hazarding the welfare of my family on a new effort as a writer. I reminded myself of my responsibilities. I accused myself of willfully entertaining a desire opposed to my responsibilities. But the effort proved fruitless. I had no greater resistance than before to this desire of writing; and the success of *Utopia* had intensified the desire by encouraging the hope that I would be successful in the future.

If I had not strength to counter the force of this desire, I had progressed sufficiently that I could admit my weakness. I had progressed sufficiently, also, to pray God for the strength I lacked, though even that effort was difficult as though I did not want Him to help—as though I wanted Him to withhold His grace and strength so that my desire would, at length, overwhelm the consciousness of my responsibility.

7

A N extraordinary number of people were present at the Cardinal's reception. They filled the Great Hall of York House and overflowed into rooms, described as "smaller," which were tremendous in themselves. Alice counted it good fortune that we found a place in the Great Hall where we could feel as though we were important participants of the event. I knew many of those present and delighted Alice by presenting her to some of famous name or large fortune; many more presented themselves to me and to Alice in tribute to my new status as author of the *Utopia*.

Cardinal Wolsey appeared, after a proper time. In scarlet robe and hat, he was an impressive figure despite his stoutness; his stoutness, in fact, seemed even to add to his impressiveness. He proceeded slowly through the crowd, his progress marked by the movement of everyone toward him that he might see and greet all of them. He had not to concern himself, as an ordinary host, with greeting his guests—those present disposed themselves that he would not fail to see and recognize them. At other times and in other places, these people might rail against him, denounce him, speak their hatred of him; here they sought his favor.

He moved slowly through the press, greeting all in his individual manner that was part graciousness and a greater part haughtiness. He was this day the most genial of men, as he could be when so disposed. Despite his gentleness of manner, none could ignore the tremendous strength and power that radiated from him as man, as cardinal, and as Lord Chancellor of England.

He greeted Alice and me in our turn. He was then most gracious. He bent his stout figure gently forward to acknowledge my wife's curtsy and smiled pleasantly at me. I was prepared to step back immediately, but he signaled me to advance another step toward him. "When this reception ends, Master More, I should like to speak with you if that will not inconvenience you." He spoke with his usual softness, but I knew that others had also heard and were astonished or envious according to their discernment of the Cardinal's purpose.

As soon as we had drawn back and His Eminence gave attention to others, my wife launched herself audibly on a series of suppositions, presentiments, deductions, and fears, which I encouraged in order to dissuade her from inquiring about my own thoughts. I had an intimation of the Cardinal's purpose, and I did not want to contemplate it; still less did I wish to share it as though the sharing would bring it nearer to reality. I felt some humor at her indignation when I seated her in one of the small rooms when the reception ended and refused to permit her to accompany me into the room where I was to meet with His Eminence.

The hour Alice was forced to remain alone in that room must have been a severe trial to her newly awakened ambitions. As soon as I reappeared, she began to ply me with questions. I increased her torments by refusing to speak of my interview with the Cardinal until we were entirely free of the building and proceeding in the carriage on the road into the city.

"You are to be knighted," she suggested when the carriage had hardly begun to move.

I laughed at the ridiculous suggestion. "And be one of King Henry's own lifeguards," I taunted.

"I trust," she said reverting to her usual severity, "that, whatever offer was made, you did not parade your silly humility before His Eminence."

"I had more income than humility to parade," I retorted.

Mistress Alice was sensitive to this inference to our worldly wealth and was shocked into momentary silence.

"His Eminence proposed to appoint me to the King's Court of Requests," I explained.

"A judge!"

"An honor without fortune," I pressed.

"You refused?" My wife was strangely indignant for a person as concerned as she with more tangible advantages.

"I told His Eminence that he was asking a tremendous sacrifice of me—of the income I receive from the law."

"And when did your income become so important to you, Master More?" she demanded.

"It is important to you," I answered.

"Your income would be repaired shortly. You know that."

"I have no desire to become involved in court intrigue," I told her.

"You still crave to give your time to writing," she said.

I should have known the impossibility of concealing myself from her penetrating eyes. "I can afford some leisure for myself," I said.

Mistress Alice's patience ended. "Why will you not put yourself forward as other men?" she demanded. "Will you sit by the fire and draw goslings in the ashes with a stick, as children do? Would God I were a man such as you! I would know what to do."

"And what would you do?"

"What! I would go forward with the best. I would rather rule than be ruled."

"You speak the truth in that," I said grimly. I was angry at her presumptuous advice; I was more angry that she had discerned my hidden desire to resume writing; I was extremely angry that this woman I had married, despite Father Paul's observation as to the opinions of my friends, had now the temerity to speak disdainfully of writing. Yet God's grace and my efforts came to my assistance in that moment of need, and I spoke none of the angry thoughts that filled my mind or the words that surged to my lips. Angry though I might be at her manner, I had still to admit her claims, as my wife and stepmother to my children, to express her views and desires.

By forcing myself to be silent through the remainder of the ride into the city, I caused Alice to become silent also. I could hold firmly to my own desire, if I wished; I could apply some of my time to writing. I reflected the irony of my situation that, having achieved sufficient literary success to justify at least partial retirement from the law I disliked, I was now offered an entirely different activity that would remove me from the law but which would also prevent me from writing. If I desired only to be free of legal activity, the Cardinal's offer would fulfill that desire. That, I knew, was insufficient.

A subsidiary advantage to a writing career would be freedom to control my life more precisely than I could while engaged in any other career. The bases of the books I would write would be religious and moral; while writing them, I would derive direct benefit from them. If they were sufficiently successful—and the certainty of success increased steadily in my mind—I would be able to apply myself ever more diligently to my spiritual life. I contemplated the possibility of scheduling my life after the manner of the Carthusians, allotting specified periods to work, others to prayer. I constructed a most attractive vision of a life dedicated to work and prayer.

I may have been deceiving myself. I may have been permitting desire to becloud judgment. I had not diminished my prayers to God for strength to resist the force of my desire; but the prospect conceived in imagination was so beguiling that I could not dispel it nor set it aside. God seemed to be withholding His assistance, and I began to anticipate that He withheld it deliberately in order to direct me toward writing.

8

A LEGAL matter intervened. Because I was proficient in both Latin and law, I was summoned to serve as interpreter to the Papal Legate, who was endeavoring to reclaim a vessel driven ashore by a gale. The vessel was the property of the Pope but, having "invaded" the realm without due permission, had been seized by the King's agents. I objected that I was not learned in maritime law, but the Legate assured me that he desired my services principally because his limited knowledge of English hampered him in the court.

Unversed as I was in law pertaining to the sea, I thought the entire matter must be quite simple. I was surprised on my first day in that court to hear lawyers of both sides advance arguments based on the most complex precedents. The case became rapidly more complicated. In turn, it also became tedious. My interest began to wane when I perceived that the lawyers of both sides seemed equally doubtful of the arguments they advanced, though they were entirely sure of the errors in their opponent's. At last, I realized that all of them were actually timid and cautious because of the exalted status of the principals.

I could not continue indefinitely as interpreter. My own work suffered. Ultimately, I became impatient and injected arguments of my own, drawn from my experience in the civil courts. The judge seemed astonished at my presumption but accepted my argument because it was not effectively countered by the lawyer for the King. Thus the case was quickly concluded by return of the vessel to the Papal Legate.

The chief lawyer for His Highness, the King, objected strenuously to the decision and, before I left the court, informed all very loudly that he would report this intrusion by a layman, as he termed me, into a matter of maritime law. His announcement amused me for the moment; a lawyer who has lost a case prefers the matter to be forgotten rather than publicized.

Two days later, however, I received a summons to present myself to His Eminence, Cardinal Wolsey, and I realized that the case of the papal vessel had become quite serious for me. Even when I presented myself, in the same room where I had talked previously with His Eminence, and saw that he welcomed me with the same graciousness as then, I was not relieved. A man of his exalted position could be gracious even when imposing most severe punishments.

"You have caused me some embarrassment, Master More," he said, and smiled.

His smile did not relieve the effect of his words on me. "I intended only to help toward conclusion of a case, Your Eminence."

My words or my expression must have told him of my alarm. My answer seemed to puzzle him momentarily so that he paused. "I am not referring to that case, Master More. I am referring to the fact that you could not agree to enter the King's service when I requested you; now His Highness demands to know why I have not enlisted you in his service."

I was tremendously relieved. "I hope that I explained sufficiently my reasons, Your Eminence."

He nodded. "And you proved me most uneconomical, Master More. I allowed you to plead that you could not afford such reduction of income when I should have offered sufficient to persuade you. Now I must explain to His Highness why a few pounds deterred me from the services of a man who has cost His Highness a fine vessel." He laughed. "Master More, His Highness was vastly amused that a layman defeated his maritime lawyers in his own court."

His reference to "a few pounds" warned me of the course of his thoughts.

"Stated in another way, Master More," he continued, "His Highness requires your services not only because he cannot afford to have you at liberty to oppose his interests, but also because he considers it improper that the author of *Utopia* is not in his service."

"I was never intended to be a courtier, Your Eminence."

"Not a courtier, Master More," he answered patiently. "His Highness has in mind that same place as Master of Requests of which I spoke with you."

"Being author of *Utopia* would not assist me to judge," I objected. I was beginning to feel somewhat desperate.

"It would add dignity to that court, Master More. Those who came to it would be assured of justice when their case was heard by the man who presented such an excellent concept of justice as you did in your book."

I was silent for the moment wondering whether I dared continue my opposition.

"Master More, may I ask why you are so determined to avoid His Highness' service?"

The question emboldened me. "You may remember, Your Eminence, that, once before, I was involved in a matter relating to a king."

He frowned immediately with distaste. "I thought all England knew that King Henry is not like his father. Master More, surely you have formed a better opinion of the King than you held of his father?"

"I have personal reasons, also, Your Eminence, that I do not feel at liberty to divulge."

Cardinal Wolsey regarded me fixedly. "Master More, it is understood in every part of the world that personal matters may never excuse a man from serving his king, his country, and his fellow men. If I remember correctly, you touched on that very subject in your book."

I felt at that moment as my father must have felt when he stood before another Lord Chancellor, Archbishop Morton. I knew I was defeated as thoroughly as my father had been. I could no longer continue opposition and objections without being disrespectful to the man who held the highest office of the Church in England and highest office of the State, after the King. As my father had been, so also was I resentful; and my resentment increased as the realization grew that His Eminence had defeated me by means of my own book as much as by use of his office.

I was dejected and intensely disappointed. The King's service would separate me from legal activities; but I would be no nearer than before to realization of my desire. Worse, I would actually suffer some loss of personal liberty in that I would come and go at the express command of the King; the external circumstances of my life would be controlled by the King instead of by me. I was not aware, at that moment, that God had chosen this peculiar manner of granting my prayer for strength. He did not give me strength; He permitted me to be overwhelmed by a superior force. I did not discern that, from the day I entered the service of the King, God would direct the external circumstances of my life under the guise of the King's directions.

I expected Alice to rejoice when I told her of my agreement to enter the King's service, but either amazement or rare perception caused her to withhold her comments. I think I should have resented, at that moment, whatever she might have said. She did not refer to the matter until the following Saturday upon her return from church.

"I no longer understand you," she announced.

I looked at her curiously, wondering what such an extraordinary admission might portend.

"I understand your ambition to write," she said. "I do not understand your willingness to enter the service of the King."

I was so astonished at her erroneous analysis that I could not speak—but she had no reason to think other than she did.

"I have been to confession this day, Master More. I have done with all the old manner of my life. I will try another manner of life, as you are trying." Her eyes lighted with their accustomed sharpness. "I will try as long as you do."

I laughed at her sudden resumption of her old character so lately discarded, but I managed to avoid any inference of derision. I did not doubt that her determination would carry her even further than I could progress. I was astonished with the knowledge that she thought I had entered voluntarily the service of the King when, actually, I had no choice, and my agreement had been a surrender rather than acceptance.

I remembered my words to Erasmus about the power of example. If ever we discussed that matter again, I should be able to expand the thesis I had outlined to him. God had forced me to be a good example to another by forcing me to accede to the King's command—an example that had proved good even when not intended to be an example. It was not my example that benefited Alice. It was the infinite power and mercy of God who had prevented me from surrendering to my desire by compelling me to enter the service of King Henry; it was the infinite power and mercy of God who made my surrender appear to be a victory in order to effect a tremendous change in Alice.

I was a little frightened at the same time by the thought that God had intervened directly in the circumstances of my life. I remembered that I had written *Utopia* to illustrate God's willingness to intervene and direct the lives of men submissive to Him; but the indication of His intervention was sufficiently frightening that I was glad to attribute the thought to a disturbed imagination, and I put it from my mind.

9

SOME weeks passed while I disengaged myself from the law by concluding cases which had been entrusted to me. At times I felt new misgivings about my entrance into the King's service; at times I almost regretted that I had not opposed the Cardinal more firmly. Much as I disliked the law, I knew the fullness of my dislike; but I knew not at all whether I should be content as servant to the King. For one cause or another, my resentment continued against His Eminence.

On the first day of service, Cardinal Wolsey's chamberlain conducted me into the presence of King Henry to pledge my fealty. We waited for a little time in an anteroom, then were ushered into a large chamber, crowded with chairs and benches and tables, and lighted by tall windows at the far end. All these physical objects diminished at the sight of the King.

Rather vaguely, I had expected him to be seated on some kind of throne from which he would look down on me kneeling before him. Instead, he stood waiting, almost in front of the tall windows, smiling graciously, as though to relieve me of that natural fear afflicting all who come before their king. Large as was the room and windows, King Henry dominated everything by his magnificent height, his bright eyes and handsome features, his athletic strength, his kingly bearing and poise. I remembered, as I walked with my escort across the room, that King Henry was but twenty-six and had not acquired those kingly virtues so evident in him. Here, indeed, was a king born. When I dropped to my knees before him, I was filled with consciousness that I was kneeling before a true king.

I raised my joined hands in front of me, but he had to lean forward slightly to take them between his own.

"Do you swear your faith to me, Master More?" he began the ritual in a clear, pleasant voice.

"I will serve thee faithfully," I answered, "in all that you entrust to me. I will be diligent, permitting nothing to delay completion of my duties. I swear unto thee my entire loyalty insofar as my conscience and the law of God permits."

His Highness released my hands and stepped backward. I remained kneeling to hear what instruction he would give.

"Master More, they serve me best who serve God first."

The unexpectedness of his thought startled me. I was prepared to hear some admonitions about my duties to protect his interests and his realm. I heard no slightest reference to anything pertaining to him. Rather did I hear words emphasizing the unfailing presence of God and the certainty of His providence.

"Look first unto God, Master More, and, after God, unto me." He turned away to the window to indicate dismissal. I had a momentary but unforgettable sight of his tall, broad-shouldered, powerful body, before the chamberlain touched my arm and drew me from the room. All my doubts and misgivings had vanished in those few minutes.

The thoughts and words of His Highness had little immediate application. As Master of his Court of Requests, I had only to determine the justice of claims presented against the Crown. All were relatively small, even insignificant to His Highness' wealth, however significant and important they were to the petitioners. Early in 1518, however, I was appointed to the council wherein were discussed all matters of importance to His Highness, and recommendations were prepared concerning the realm. I attended several sessions without offering comment—indeed, for the most part, the Cardinal both presided and directed all proceedings within the council, obviating the necessity for comments or suggestions by others. In addition, as the only commoner in that group of clergy and nobles, and having the least experience, I was reluctant to thrust myself into prominence.

In the spring of that year, Cardinal Wolsey proposed a recommendation before the council that King Henry appoint a new official, a Chief Constable of the realm. Certainly there was need for an arresting officer who, representing the King's own power, would not fear to arrest even the greatest noble for violating the law of the realm.

"There is one practical difficulty," His Eminence elaborated. "Of those who might be nominated, I can think of none among the nobles or clergy who would be willing to assume such an onerous task. Until we determine one who is fitted both by temperament and experience, I will assume the position myself."

I waited expectantly, but no one spoke. The nobles present seemed tense but unwilling to speak; the members of the clergy were uninterested. To me, the proposal was preposterous; yet I hesitated to speak when all others were silent. Then I remembered the King's own words, "Look first unto God." I could not, with good conscience, refuse to challenge the Cardinal's proposal, which seemed so dangerous to justice.

"Your Eminence," I protested, "as Lord Chancellor, you are the highest judge. If you also become the highest arresting officer, whatever man you arrest will be adjudged guilty even before his trial." I was startled at the anger that appeared suddenly in Cardinal Wolsey's expression. I was conscious also that some of the nobles had stirred and that some of the clergy had turned to look at me.

"Master More"—the Cardinal spoke sharply—"you are a fool."

I sensed too late that I had become involved in some issue, the true dimensions of which I was ignorant and from which I must escape as quickly and unobtrusively as possible. "Thank God His Highness has but one in his Council," I answered. I was tremendously relieved that the others laughed and thus closed the encounter. Still, I regretted that I had antagonized His Eminence, for, despite memory of the King's words, I was mindful of the Cardinal's power.

Not many days later, when I was summoned to the presence of the Lord Chancellor, I responded with a willingness more apparent than real. I dreaded what he had devised as retribution. Nor was I reassured by the seriousness of his expression when I stood before him. He was no longer angry and motioned that I should be seated; but I could derive little comfort from such outward signs.

"Master More, when first I invited you to enter the service of the King, you refused. You agreed to enter his service only when the King himself required it. Because of that, I entertained the thought that you were entirely a King's man."

"I am, Your Eminence," I affirmed quickly.

The Cardinal wagged his head disapprovingly. "You are also singularly innocent, Master More, for one who is a councilor to His Highness."

I did not understand him and remained silent.

"You are a lawyer, Master More, so you are familiar with 'lawyers' envy.' Perhaps you know better than I how lawyers covet positions in the service of His Highness and to what extent they envy the clergy who hold those positions. Have you not observed that another class of society is equally envious and even more anxious to supplant the clergy in the service of His Highness?"

I knew then that he was referring to the nobles. That knowledge informed me also that his proposal of a Chief Constable was directed entirely against the nobles. That did not vitiate the strength of my objection, however. If a man is arrested by the judge who will preside at the trial, either that man is guilty, or the judge is a man of rare justice.

"I am not disagreeing with the objection you stated," His Eminence said, anticipating me. "But you must know, Master More, that the King will never be secure on his throne as long as there are men sufficiently powerful to defy the officers and courts of his realm. The clergy are loyal to him as he is good to them. Their attention is not divided between his interests and their own ambitions. Neither do they go about divulging to others secret matters of the King or the State. That cannot be said of others; His Highness knows that he cannot trust those others. You must know that also, Master More. Now that you are informed I hope that, in the future, the interests of His Highness will guide your attitude."

I perceived nothing to be gained by telling the consideration that had led me to oppose his proposal. He knew the principles of His Highness as well as I knew the one His Highness had told me. At the moment, my dominant desire was merely to be excused lest the Cardinal's anger revive.

I was not at all sure that it had disappeared as completely as his manner indicated. I had not yet learned that His Eminence could become angry when opposed yet, after a little time, admit the correctness of opposition if it contained nothing of malice.

As though to convince me of his good will, he appointed my father, shortly after, as a judge of the King's bench. I could not misunderstand his action: He wanted me to be not only a "King's man" but a "Cardinal's man" also. I was grateful to His Eminence for this kindness to my father; but I did not permit gratitude to interfere with a decision I made that, in all matters, I should do as the King had commanded—"look first unto God." I would support the Cardinal's proposals or oppose them as my conscience directed. In that I would have the sure protection of King Henry.

His Eminence made no other effort to enlist me to his group and, after a time, I felt content that he respected my position as "King's man" and was satisfied that I had no tendency to join another group. Some months later, however, I realized that he had not lost interest in me, for I was then relieved of my duties in the Court of Requests and appointed secretary to King Henry.

His Highness himself selected me as the man he desired in that position, but I knew he would not appoint me without approval of the Cardinal. None at court was closer to the King than his secretary, none had greater opportunity to plead causes for themselves or their friends, none enjoyed greater trust and confidence, none were more generously rewarded by His Highness. Cardinal Wolsey had approved me, I knew, because I was devoted to the King; perhaps he hoped, also, that I should be influenced to greater sympathy for his interests. I contented myself with being grateful to him.

10

THE first tribute to my influential position came from the King's own Chief Justice, who asked that I accept his grandson in my service. The boy was nineteen, considerably older than I had been when I was placed in the service of Archbishop Morton, but desired service in my home because of love for literature. Thus, William Roper joined my family. He was inclined to dullness, and I saw little possibility that he would ever succeed in literature; but he had been trained also in law and was well mannered, so that he was entirely agreeable to Alice and my children.

The good fortune of my new position as secretary of His Highness was marred by return of the plague that had claimed the life of Middleton eleven years earlier. As soon as King Henry learned that the plague had returned, the entire court transferred from London to Woking, then to a series of other locations. As a result, I was separated from my family throughout that summer and subjected to fears for their safety.

That plague did have a beneficial effect, however, on King Henry and members of the court by causing renewed emphasis on spiritual life and spiritual matters. Balls, banquets, and other frivolous amusements diminished in number, first as a result of confusion attendant on frequent moves from one location to another, later because of greater attention to the spirit. King Henry and Queen Catherine provided the example, and all of the court imitated them.

Even in daily affairs of State, King Henry displayed an unusual consciousness of the presence of God. Often, while giving me instructions, his conversation would turn from the subject and progress into spiritual matters.

I was not deluded in believing that I was witnessing a mass conversion from the world to God. In the forty-one years of my life, I had seen many similar outbursts of fervor among the common people and had indulged in some myself. I did see in this that God was again using tribulation and anxiety as His device for calling men closer to Himself. Men who can forget Him readily in times of prosperity return quickly to Him in times of adversity. A renewal of piety therefore, was not extraordinary; continuation of piety when adversity had passed would be extraordinary.

That period of danger wrought a change in King Henry more marked than in the others. When the plague had passed, he did not resume again his addiction to amusements and gambling. Rather was he a model to all others of the court, attending numerous Masses and other devotions.

Following closely the end of the plague came news that an Augustinian monk in Germany, a Martin Luther, had both lost his own faith and was engaged in despoiling the common people of theirs. King Henry himself explained the man's heresy, the protection he enjoyed from some avaricious nobles, and the errors—according to reason and Scripture—on which the man based his novel doctrines.

There were some among those gathered to hear King Henry who scoffed at his "preaching," derided his piety, and laughed at his vanity. He said nothing publicly against these, properly restricting his confidences to his confessor; but, with little warning, he dispatched many of those who had been his more intimate companions to posts in Calais and Guines and to distant places in England. His action convinced those who remained that King Henry had begun a new manner of life.

One apparent defect troubled me. I had not forgotten Father Paul's admonition of prayer and fasting as the beginning of spiritual life. I saw abundant evidence of prayer and devotion by the King; I saw none of fasting and mortification even when specifically required by commandment of the Church.

I did not presume to criticize. Neither did I consider myself sufficiently experienced in spiritual matters to regard this single defect as serious. I was no more than troubled by omission of what Father Paul had designated as requisite, and I countered my troubled feeling with the hope that God drew different men by different ways.

From that time, His Highness began to enter into discussions with me, most frequently about the Sacraments and the teaching of Aquinas—of whom I knew little, preferring the more agreeable literary style of St. Augustine—and of the heretical mouthings of Luther. I enjoyed those discussions in the privacy of the King's study. I learned that he enjoyed them the more when I assumed the role of heretic myself, thus taxing him to greater thought and precise answers. Whenever he discovered an irrefutable counter to my arguments, he smiled delightedly.

"More," His Highness announced at the end of one session, "I am of a mind to incorporate my thoughts in a book as an answer to this stupid Luther."

"None other can do it as effectively as Your Highness," I said.

He laughed loudly. "You have become a flattering courtier, More," he said.

"I was referring to your position as much as to your ability, Your Highness. If Luther finds his protection among the petty princes and avaricious nobles of Germany, who will uncover him more effectively than the King of England? I meant no flattery, Your Highness," I continued seriously. "I think that the whole world benefits when the leaders of men lead the way toward God."

He did not laugh again. He thought for a time, and his thoughts were sufficiently pleasant that his smile remained constant. He brought his open hand heavily down on the desk before him. "I will do it, More! I will write the answer. You will say nothing of what claims my attention. When I am finished, I shall have the celebrated author of *Utopia* edit my work."

Remembering my own inability to divide attention between legal matters and writing, I was amazed by King Henry's ability to attend to his duties of State and, concluding them, turn immediately to his book. I had regarded myself and been regarded by others as unusually gifted; I was humbled by the remarkable ability of my King, thirteen years my junior.

The completed work, when he gave it to me, delighted me from the beginning, astonished me as I proceeded. Men need not be scholars to read and understand the King's words and thoughts; yet scholars would learn much from the book. I could find only one item to question, and that as to prudence rather than matter.

"I would ask you to review again this one point, Your Highness, where you refer to the temporal power of the Pope."

His Highness' expression became grave as soon as I mentioned that one point, and he seemed about to halt any objection, but then signified that I might continue.

"It may happen at some future time that disagreement will rise, as does sometimes happen between Christian princes; for the Pope is both spiritual and temporal ruler, and it is possible that temporal interests may inspire some conflict. If I be permitted to suggest, Your Highness, I favor that the point be eliminated altogether or, at the least, touched more lightly."

He shook his head emphatically. "I will not diminish that in the slightest, More. I am indebted to His Holiness' temporal power even for this throne. Shall I demonstrate my gratitude by denying that power?" He stood up as though he were so annoyed that he could not bear my effrontery. "Who might now be King of England had not Pope Innocent confirmed my father to the throne?"

"I was not informed of that, Your Highness," I said.

He recovered his humor quickly and even read again that section to which I had objected. When he finished, he put the pages of the manuscript together, indicating by his action that the matter was concluded. "You found little to challenge, More," he said with a laugh. I could understand that part of his pleasure arose from my reputation as a learned man, in that he had demonstrated his superiority and forced me to recognize it. I was slightly dismayed to have recalled to me the memory of Grocyn. I was elated, at the same time, to know that even this point of the Pope's temporal power was well founded.

I benefited exceedingly as a result of the objection that had aroused His Highness. Had I approved without objection all that he had written, he might well have suspected me as a courtier; I had objected to that point which he seemed to esteem above all others, and his reaction was the more pronounced. I received, of his generosity, some lands in the country, which almost doubled my income.

The work had far greater effect than even I had prophesied when His Highness first proposed it. England's pride in her King was multiplied by this evidence of his learning and virtue. Scholars of Europe either praised the book extravagantly or denounced it in such terms as to prove its worth. In Germany, Martin Luther was led to expose his depraved soul by an intemperate attack; and shortly after, the peasants, robbed of their faith by this man, rose up in rebellion against him. From Rome came the greatest mark of worth: Pope Leo dispatched a cardinal to bring to King Henry a new and cherished title, "Defender of the Faith."

His Highness had watched anxiously, as all authors must, the reception of his work. As reports mounted, his interest veered from initial anxiety to satisfaction, then to wonder. He had not expected such acclaim. He was tremendously elated, not as king, but as author. He was transported with delight with the title "Defender of the Faith," which raised him to equality in the Papal Court with the Kings of France and Spain. In the elation of the moment, he professed increased appreciation for my arguments that had inspired him to the work and for my efforts as editor, and transferred to me more lands by which I became truly a landed gentleman.

Wealth had lost its attraction, I realized. I felt no elation at these gifts or my new status. That disinterest was not of my doing, I knew. I had no greater power than any man to become poor in spirit; but God worked in me that great mystery of love in which, possessing all things, I used them as though I possessed them not at all. I was happy—grateful to God for the gifts He showered on me, more grateful to Him for having placed me in the service of this virtuous and learned king.

11

OTHERS were more impressed than I by my favor with His Highness. Inspired by the example of my king, I began to write a new work of my own, a treatise on death, judgment, heaven, and hell. Almost immediately after, death caused the vacancy of the office of Undertreasurer of the Realm, and I was appointed to the vacancy, terminating my new literary effort as though God did not wish me to be attracted again toward writing.

The appointment itself astonished me. It necessitated that I be knighted by King Henry, an honor not lightly conferred by him. More remarkable, it necessitated approval by the Treasurer of the Realm, Lord Norfolk, who should have selected his assistant from among the nobles at court of whom he was the leader, or from among commoners identified with the nobles.

As Master in the King's Court of Requests and as secretary to His Highness, I had been employed in positions that protected me, by their very function, from identification with either the Cardinal's adherents at court or the nobles. Those positions demanded complete attention to the wishes and interests of King Henry, an impossibility had I permitted myself to advance my own interests or another's. I was known to all as a "King's man," completely separate from the two groups identified either with the Cardinal or with Lord Norfolk.

That I was now chosen to be Undertreasurer and knighted—I became Sir Thomas and was no longer Master More—indicated that the nobles wished to include me in their group but also plunged me into the plots and counter-plots and intrigue which are the common activities of those surrounding the King. I determined that I would be no more identified with them than I had been with the adherents of the Cardinal; yet I anticipated that I would have difficulty. Lord Norfolk, a dark, serious, intense man, coveting for himself the place held by Cardinal Wolsey, would not be content while I remained only a "King's man"; he would press constantly to make me a "nobles' man."

Relations between the two groups made my position extremely difficult from the beginning. I was hardly installed as Undertreasurer when a court of nobles, presided over by Lord Norfolk, sentenced the Duke of Buckingham to execution for treason. In public and in the privacy of the room assigned to me as Undertreasurer, Lord Norfolk raged that all was done by Cardinal Wolsey.

"His Eminence had the man arrested. His Eminence supplied the evidence," he protested to me. His voice was husky, whether from rage or grief I could not tell. "The man is my father-in-law, but His Eminence made me preside over that court."

If I was impressed by his sincerity, I was mindful that he could have cried out to the King against the injustice he pleaded before me. He walked fitfully about the room in front of me, crossing from the window on one side to stand for a moment before the window at the other. He was slight of build, so that his nervousness was the more apparent. I could not escape the impression that some part of his nervousness arose from guilt.

"The evidence was conclusive, My Lord," I offered.

He swung around. "Buckingham himself protested his innocence, Sir Thomas. Does a man lie when he stands on the very threshold of eternity?"

"Men can delude themselves."

He walked angrily across the room and stood looking out vacantly.

"His Highness would not have permitted execution were he not convinced by evidence," I added confidently. King Henry's devotion to God and conscience was sufficiently known to justify my statement.

Lord Norfolk hurried back across the room to lean belligerently across my desk and put his face very close to mine. "You are a known 'King's man,' Sir Thomas; but you know how easily His Eminence influences King Henry."

The accusation astounded me. In the time while I had served as secretary to His Highness, I had seen many letters from His Eminence to the King and had written as many for the King to His Eminence. Not once did I remember that His Eminence had opposed the King; many times I remembered when the King opposed or modified some measure proposed by the Cardinal. To me, Lord Norfolk's accusation was incredible; but he left my room so quickly after his statement that I had no opportunity to reply.

The execution of the Duke of Buckingham became a public issue, partly because of the bravery of the man, partly because of his repeated claims of innocence, partly because of those interested in discrediting the Cardinal and the clergy. In my own home, the youthful Roper reflected public indignation by virtually repeating the charges against Cardinal Wolsey that I had heard from Lord Norfolk.

"You have heard but one of the litigants, Son Roper,"

I cautioned him. "You are sufficiently versed in law to know that the judge must hear the defendant as well as the plaintiff."

The youth was versed in law but not in men and waved my comment aside. "The Duke of Buckingham insisted that he was innocent. Lord Norfolk said that the Cardinal was responsible. Shall we say that the one man died with a lie on his lips and the other is continuing the lie?"

"We should do well to say nothing of the matter whatever," I answered shortly. I was exhausted with the subject and saw that Roper's youthfulness would not permit him to believe that men can deceive themselves for their purposes.

"Nothing but the Cardinal's vainglory, his ambition and his avarice are responsible for this," Roper declared.

He would have continued to unknown lengths of condemnation, but I raised my hand to ask silence. "Let me enjoy peace here within my home, Son Roper," I said.

Despite the proofs, available to all, of the executed Duke's guilt, the gigantic lie against His Eminence proved superior—not that any thought the Duke innocent, but because many wanted to believe His Eminence guilty of this heinous charge. As the lie gained credence, I expected His Eminence to denounce it and its inventors. He did nothing, seemingly unaware of the lie, unaware that the lie was believed by the common people because of his silence, unaware that the lawyers had seized upon it eagerly to denounce him publicly and discredit all of the clergy and the Church.

I had occasion to visit him soon after in the privacy of his study with papers that required his signature and the Great Seal. He gave no outward indication of being perturbed; he was fully as pleasant as he always was whenever we met.

I hesitated for some moments but could not lose the opportunity. "May I speak, Your Eminence, of a matter resulting from the execution of the Duke of Buckingham?"

He glanced up from the papers I had delivered. "You are concerned about the reaction, Sir Thomas?"

"I am concerned about the manner some are making use of his execution to the detriment of the clergy and the Church."

He lifted his hand lightly as though dismissing something negligible. "It will exhaust itself."

"In time," I agreed, "but the present damage is considerable."

"Denials will accomplish nothing," he answered decisively.

"Your own reputation is suffering, Your Eminence," I protested.

He was genuinely amused. "My day-to-day reputation with the people is unimportant. My reputation with the King is important. Sir Thomas, if I attempted to defend myself against all the canards circulated about me, I should have no time to do anything else."

I could not revert again to the discredit attaching to the clergy and the Church. His complacency puzzled me and troubled me, but I could do nothing more. Pride made him contemptuous of his enemies' efforts and equally contemptuous of the opinion of the people.

Popular hostility against the Cardinal declined slowly despite the efforts of London lawyers to sustain it. The common people could not maintain their indignation without fresh material, and none could be manufactured; the Duke of Buckingham receded slowly from public memory. Strife between the faction of Cardinal Wolsey and the nobles led by Norfolk seemed also to diminish, and such troubles as appeared were minor in nature and limited to disagreements between subordinate persons.

In the spring of 1522, Cardinal Wolsey himself abruptly ended the apparent truce between his group and the nobles. During a reception at York House, when guests filled the Great Hall, the Cardinal's voice suddenly rose so that it could be heard by everyone.

"You have been meeting secretly one of the Queen's young ladies, boy. What interest could you have in Lady Anne Boleyn?"

Everyone present stood rigidly still and silent at mention of the name of Lord Norfolk's niece. Everyone present knew they were witnessing resumption of the feud between the Cardinal and the leader of the nobles. At the moment, however, few understood the significance of the Cardinal's attack since the boy who grew pale and trembled before him was heir to the Duke of Northumberland.

"I marvel, boy," the Cardinal continued in a loud voice, "that you so forget the great family to which you were born—or that you would dare to act as you have without permission of the King nor even of your father."

Distraught to learn that his meetings with Lady Anne had been discovered, or by the sharpness of the Cardinal's words, the boy cried openly. "The woman who mastered me is not a foolish girl, Your Eminence," he protested. "Lady Anne is Norfolk blood, equal to me in birth and almost equal in estate."

Without so intending and striving only to defend his love, the youth's blundering words revealed the whole justification of the Cardinal's attack—a marriage union of this youthful Northumberland with Lady Anne Boleyn would bring into closer union the three greatest families in England: Norfolk, Northumberland, and Buckingham. That would be a union dangerous not alone to the Cardinal but even to King Henry.

By one stroke, His Eminence crushed his opponents. The youthful Northumberland's father came to London—a humiliating journey—to conduct his son to the north country, and he reproached Norfolk bitterly as having promoted the attachment between his son and Norfolk's niece, Lady Anne. After this, the heirs of Buckingham, awakening to knowledge they had chosen previously to ignore, publicly accused Norfolk of having pronounced the sentence of death despite the innocence of the accused. By the simple expedient of exposing, in violent terms, an innocent love between a boy and a girl, His Eminence had divided and crushed his enemies.

12

A T the time, the conflict between the Cardinal and nobles seemed not to involve me. I had avoided identification with the nobles as I had avoided identification with the adherents of the Cardinal. Death of the Duke of Buckingham, humiliation of Northumberland, and discrediting of Lord Norfolk all strengthened my determination to avoid partisanship or identification with any faction. I was secure in the affections of the King; I was ambitious only to serve him by performing my duties.

When the court was in London, I was able to enjoy my leisure with my family. On those occasions, so filled was I with pleasure to be away from the court, that I did not observe (until Alice compelled me) the mutual interest of my Margaret and William Roper. I observed it, in fact, only just in time to avoid being taken by surprise when Margaret, first, then Roper, asked permission to marry. I welcomed their marriage. If young Roper was without humor and somewhat dull, he was not different from the law students I remembered; and he was morally upright.

Their marriage was not equal in splendor to some marriages I had attended during my years at court; yet it was satisfying to me, father of the bride, and more so to my father. I had climbed to such tremendous height in worldly affairs that my daughter could marry the grandson of the King's Chief Justice; and young Roper's family congratulated themselves that their son was marrying the daughter of the King's Undertreasurer. The church could not contain all those of our friends—members of the court, nobles, commoners, and clergy, the great of the city, merchants, and that small group known simply as the learned. King Henry and Queen Catherine also sent a present so that my favor with them would be evidenced.

None of this was unusual, nothing extraordinary. All seemed to follow the pattern of life normal to rich and poor. Yet by such normal and ordinary events does God direct us. Young Roper was more distant even than I from the conflict between Cardinal and nobles at court; yet through him did I learn that the rivalry between them was begun again, more subtly, more viciously, more bitterly than before. Through him was I directed into later events of my own life.

I was not immediately aware of a relationship between that strife and my son-in-law: I noticed nothing more than Roper's increasing criticism of priests and their actions, a criticism that was merely an extension of his solemn rectitude. He and my Margaret were married a full year—I waited each day my first grandchild—before the stature of Roper's criticisms impressed me, and I answered him seriously, rather than humorously as had been my custom.

"Men begin against the clergy, Son Roper, but end by throwing themselves against the whole Church."

He answered me with such an ill-tempered tirade against clergy and those who respected the office of the priesthood that I became angry also. "Soon you will cry with those others to cast out the clergy that the gospel may be preached. Who will preach it? Who but some Lutherans! And what will be their gospel? Not your gospel of Christ.

No! Luther's gospel that faith is sufficient and good works without merit—that the sacraments count for nothing and purgatory does not exist . . ."

"He can correct those mistakes later," he answered stubbornly.

The stupidity of his answer made me aware of my anger as an intelligent answer could not; made me realize that I was not so much angry that he defended Luther as I was at his defiant refusal to submit to me. I tried to devise some statement that would at least turn him away from the path he followed. But I could not trust myself to speak moderately. I made no answer, but left him. Further argument would serve only to force him into new errors, new stupidities. I would argue with him no more: I would content myself with prayer that God would restore to him his faith.

Prayer seemed unavailing. The encounter between us had inflamed him; my abrupt departure convinced him that I was unable to counter him. Soon I was summoned by Cardinal Wolsey and told that Roper was speaking his heresies publicly and, if he continued, would be summoned before a court.

"He is your son-in-law, Sir Thomas," His Eminence prompted.

"I can do nothing with him," I admitted. "I antagonized him by turning my anger against him."

"Send him to me! I will tell him he will be arrested and tried if he continues."

I felt faint at the prospect presented by the threat. "If he is like the rest of the heretics, Your Eminence, he will welcome the notoriety of martyrdom."

Cardinal Wolsey considered momentarily. Then a small, amused smile broke the sternness of his expression.

"Then, Sir Thomas, suppose I tell him that he will not be arrested—that we consider him as one of those poor unfortunates who are allowed to preach what they please because we know them to be addled?"

I had no hope that the remedy would be effective; but I remembered how effectively this prelate had crushed his enemies. For myself, I concentrated the more on prayer.

Son Roper reacted furiously and with greater industry to the words of the Cardinal. He refused to join in our prayers, refused any longer to attend Mass, ranted intemperately of priests and bishops and cardinals whenever I was present, endeavoring to goad me to reply. I was humiliated to learn that he had increased his public activities also and became so bold as to preach his heresies to the common people in the streets of the city.

God must have given me freely of His grace during those tormented days. Each new outburst by my son-in-law in my presence, each new report of his public activities, revived my anger. I had determined not to answer his stupidities, but I was often tempted to denounce him. With God's grace, I restrained myself and held stubbornly to silence in his presence and steadfastly to prayer.

I will not contend that God heard my prayer. If, in fact, He did, He adopted a wondrous strange and ridiculous means of granting it. Son Roper preached in public so vehemently and at such length that even the dullest of the common people saw that the Cardinal and clergy regarded him as addled and listened to him no more. I began to receive reports that, when he attempted to preach, those passing by taunted him without stopping to hear him. When the boy could endure no more their humiliations, he ceased his utterances.

For some time, he was silent at home as he was in public. Then, without explaining, he returned to church, to confession, and to Christ's own Blessed Sacrament. One fault remained to him ever after that: He never forgave Cardinal Wolsey for the compassion that had deprived him of the martyrdom for which he thirsted!

I was indebted to His Eminence, not alone for his solution to the issue, but also his forbearance; but the Cardinal brushed aside my expression of gratitude. "If I were entitled to gratitude or payment, Sir Thomas, I have already received them in far greater abundance than would be possible to you. Did you wonder at the boy's learning or where he acquired such sudden brilliance of mind?" He walked to a cabinet, drew a key from his robe as though he had been unwilling to entrust it to any other, opened the doors, and drew from the interior a heavy bundle of printed pamphlets which he placed before me. "There, Sir Thomas, are young Roper's sources of wisdom. In the heat of his temper, he told me of some—told me enough that I knew where to send for the rest."

The address of the printer at the bottom of each pamphlet made his meaning clear. Germany! "Your Eminence, the King's men at the ports would prevent entry of this material into the country," I objected.

"King's men—yes," he agreed. "Men thirsting for the King's favor would be happy to permit entry. They hope to destroy Wolsey, Sir Thomas. To do it, they are willing to destroy the Church."

"Some, Your Eminence," I objected, "but surely not all."

The Cardinal shook his head irritably. "Some or all, Sir Thomas! The number is unimportant when they are the most powerful of all." He looked at me closely. "Is it difficult to believe, Sir Thomas, that men would destroy the Church for their own gain?"

I could not agree with him, but I was indebted to him for his mercy to Son Roper and could not openly contradict him.

"Search for yourself, Sir Thomas," he burst out savagely. "Learn for yourself how easily the people of London can acquire these." He waved his arm above the pamphlets heaped on his desk. "Decide for yourself what power caused these to be admitted past the King's men at the ports."

I had no trouble confirming all that he told me. I visited sufficient of the printers I knew, found each engaged in selling pamphlets similar to those in the possession of the Cardinal, and learned how easily they had obtained them from men who had brought them past the King's men at the ports. I could no longer doubt that powerful men had arranged all—men who were willing to destroy the Church for their own gain.

13

THE succession of events alerted me. The encounter with Son Roper and consciousness of my anger at his defiance warned me against complacency of the spirit. Confirmation of the Cardinal's words warned me against the deceptiveness of others. I desired nothing so much as to be completely free of the court and its intrigues. I would have cared not at all if I had been returned once again to the practice of law; even that would have been a safe refuge from the conflict. But I had begged God to release me from that life of bickering and disputes about money and rights; I accepted the life I had and begged His protection.

Outwardly, I had neither care for the present nor anxiety for the future. Wealth and honors flowed into my hands without interruption. When I served as ambassador for the King, all circumstances joined toward success. His Highness appointed me High Steward of Oxford and, soon after, of Cambridge. I built a great house at Chelsea, just west of the city, where I could live with my wife and my children, my father, the young men entrusted to my service, and the young Anne Cresacre, who was my ward. I was the master of many servants, and I had a barge with bargemen to row me to the city each morning and return me when the day's work ended. When my daughters Elizabeth and Cecily married, they married two of the young men in my service, both of good family and some estate. My son, John, married Anne Cresacre. For a time, His Highness came often to visit me, to walk with me in my garden, to talk with me, and to laugh with me. My house in Chelsea was a dreamworld of happiness.

Inwardly, I did not see these things as others might. I saw and became increasingly more conscious that one thing was lacking from this vision of perfection. I had no cross. I was mindful that all that men called mine was God's gift— His trust to me. I prayed diligently; I fasted as I always had. Often I wondered that I did not do more, but always I comforted myself that I did as much as God gave me to do. I was not more attached to my material possessions and assured myself that I could part from them without distress. Yet I had no cross, and I was conscious that, without a cross, I felt far from Christ; without a cross, I might easily permit fortune to lull me from watchfulness.

In 1525, when I was forty-seven, His Highness elevated me to a new honor, taking me from the position as Under-treasurer and making me Chancellor of his own Archduchy of Lancaster. As before, I knew that I was again indebted to His Eminence, the Cardinal, for this position; but I no longer sought his motive as I had in the past when I suspected that he wanted to number me among his group. He had brought me into the service of the King, had approved me as secretary to His Highness, had been kind to my father and merciful to Son Roper; not once had he asked of me anything more than continued loyalty to the King.

At the same time, His Highness named as Earl of Wiltshire one Thomas Boleyn, and the pleasure I might have felt in my new appointment was vitiated by this other. The man had served the King as ambassador but had never distinguished himself. More significant was his position as brother-in-law of Lord Norfolk and father of the "foolish girl," Lady Anne. The title given the man was indicative of much or revealing of much that I did not want to contemplate.

The King himself was brooding and moody, preoccupied, seemingly uncertain about decisions. He took no more pleasure in discussions; often he did no more than nod recognition when I came before him with some business of the archduchy. I attributed his attitude to indisposition, but I could not avoid recognizing a relation between his attitude and the honor accorded the father of Lady Anne.

Two more years passed, their even flow undisturbed by trouble or problem. In 1527, I learned of the King's scrupulous anxiety about the validity of his marriage to Queen Catherine. Remembering my own ordeal of fears, I sympathized with him and prayed that he would soon be delivered from those torments. Many other events must have happened during that fateful year of which I know nothing; I know only that, with others, I was aware of the Cardinal's loss of King Henry's favor and of Lady Anne's gradual emergence as the one who supplanted the Cardinal. How this matter came about, I know not; my mind reverts insistently to the love between Lady Anne and the youthful Northumberland and to the accusation of the boy's father that Lord Norfolk had promoted that love.

Late in that year of 1527, when all knew that Cardinal Wolsey had lost the favor of His Highness to Lady Anne, I felt the first uneasiness in some years. It was not spiritual in nature; it was merely an alerting to the personal danger of involvement in the Great Matter of the King. I sensed that greater safety lay in complete avoidance of the matter, and

I refused to discuss with others the validity of the marriage of King Henry and Queen Catherine. I asserted to any who introduced the subject that I was not qualified to express opinion on a matter so vast and complicated.

I admit now that I was moved less by humility, as I protested, than by prudence. I assured myself that I did well to leave the subject entirely to the Cardinal and bishops then studying it. Whenever I found myself occupied with considerations about it, I thrust them from my mind. If I refused to consider the King's Great Matter, I could not form an opinion about it, could say honestly that I held no opinion, and could escape whatever danger might attach to an opinion.

God would not permit my evasion. In 1528, Bishop Tunstall of London authorized me to read the heretical pamphlets flooding into the country from Germany that I might refute them with books of my own. It was an extraordinary license to be granted a layman and was granted principally because many of the pamphlets attacked the clergy and could be answered more effectively by a layman. Others, however, including the King, interpreted the license as indication that I was learned in theology.

I was discussing with the King some matter of the archduchy when he suddenly pushed aside the papers of the case and asked abruptly my opinion of the royal marriage.

"My opinion would be of little consequence, Your Highness. I have given the matter no thought." I was, for the moment, well satisfied with the security conferred by my ignorance.

His Highness drew toward him a great Bible from which markers projected. He opened the sacred book at one of the places. "He that marrieth his brother's wife, doth an unlawful thing, he hath uncovered his brother's nakedness: they shall be without children," he read from Leviticus. "There, More. The word of God is sufficiently clear."

His resort to the Bible alarmed me; that was the way of the Lutherans—taking one verse of the holy words to support what they wished to believe rather than to believe what God intended to teach. It was a method calculated to convince unlearned men or men as stupid as my son Roper. But I could not regard the King as unlearned nor as suffering the stupidity of Roper. I returned to the refuge of my claimed ignorance. "Your Highness, so little do I know of this great matter that I thought the question was founded entirely on some apparent defect in the Bull of Dispensation."

The King straightened as though wearied by the cares and fears that claimed him. "That was the beginning. It is of minor importance. It is clear now that His Holiness has not power to dispense this impediment established by God Himself. Is not His prohibition plainly stated?"

"A brother's wife is not a brother's widow, Your Highness," I resorted to his own method of argument. "Without studying the matter, I think the words apply only to the taking of a living brother's wife, for that certainly would be wrong."

King Henry raised his hand irritably. "You are quibbling, More. God's words are not to be restricted and limited to fit whatever circumstances we wish. Study the matter, More. Discuss it with Master Foxe. Then tell me your views."

So commanded, I could no longer continue to take refuge in ignorance. I sought Master Foxe for discussion, and I studied the matter as much as I was able, despite my lack of training in such subjects and lack of books to guide me. Dominant in my mind was the memory of the King's book defending the sacraments, his learning in the theology of Aquinas, the study he had given to this present matter. He was better able than I to search this subject.

Despite all my efforts and my respect for the King's learning, I could find my way to but one conclusion: that Holy Mother Church and His Holiness had full authority for the dispensation granted King Henry to marry his brother's widow, Queen Catherine. Tactfully and circumspectly, I recited to His Highness my inability to think differently about the matter from how I had thought before. I was apprehensive that he would question me and force me to express myself in direct opposition to the views he had already stated; but he indicated little interest and soon dismissed me. I was greatly relieved. I resumed my former attitude of careful avoidance of his Great Matter.

The King's personal problem overshadowed all else. Throughout England, men proclaimed their views—commoners as readily as nobles and clergy. King Henry found support and defense among the nobles and London lawyers, little among the clergy and commoners. In all sections was heard sympathy and support for Queen Catherine, condemnation of Lady Anne, and ribald laughter at the King's conscience. So sure was the common mind that King Henry only wanted excuse for his passion that, when an ecclesiastical court was summoned to hear the case, disturbances occurred throughout the country.

Cardinal Wolsey was named by Rome as one of the judges. A great outcry of protest greeted that announcement, so well had nobles and lawyers turned the common mind against him. Commoners pretended to see in that appointment sure indication that the royal marriage would be annulled. Their resentment was such that when the second judge, Cardinal Campeggio, arrived from Rome, the commoners cried out against him as he rode into the city.

For myself, I was happy that an embassy removed me from the country at the very time the marriage court assembled; and this once I did not hurry the business entrusted to me. Couriers arriving with papers and instructions informed me of the progress of the trial—from Queen Catherine's appeal to the gallantry of the King to the astonishing news that the court had recessed without giving judgment.

I was tremendously relieved. So sure had been everyone in England—even in Europe—that Cardinal Wolsey favored annulment of the royal marriage that my confidence in him had weakened. All England and all Europe were amazed, for few had attributed to him the courage necessary to withstand the King. So long had his name been identified with the interests of King Henry that men had forgotten that he was a Prince of the Church.

That the nobles had triumphed over the Cardinal was evident on every side when I returned again to England. King Henry had retired to the country, surrounded now entirely by nobles. Of the clergy, only some priest-chaplains accompanied him. The Cardinal remained in London, still Lord Chancellor but knowing, as did everyone, that he had lost all favor. I was told immediately that power rested with the nobles—especially with the brother of Lady Anne. In mid-October, Cardinal Wolsey was indicted in King's Court, King Henry reclaimed the Great Seal, and Cardinal Wolsey was no longer Lord Chancellor.

14

I SECLUDED myself in my great house at Chelsea, trying to distract myself by the pleasure of being with my family and staying long hours in my chapel. Few came to visit me during that time, and those few explained why more did not. A pall of gloom, of uneasiness, of dread descended over all England. Men knew not what to expect. The great Cardinal who had been most favored of the King, he who had been Lord Chancellor for the long space of seventeen years, was now accused of violating the King's own laws.

A summons from His Highness forced me from my refuge. With great display of promptness, but with a most grievous interior reluctance, I presented myself before him in London. I was fearful of his purpose. I had been always a "King's man," but some had also called me a "Cardinal's man."

Months had passed since I last saw His Highness, at the time I departed on the embassy. Then, he had been downcast and heavy of spirit; now he was the spirited and gracious prince I had known in the early years of my service to him, and I felt better at sight of him. He was decisive in manner and action so that my spirits rose higher at these evidences of his recovery. His expression revealed but one mark of his trials—he had not recovered his gaiety, and there was attached to him an indication of serious and intent purpose that was almost grimness.

"More, you have given thought to my Great Matter?"

His words stopped the rapid rise of my spirits. I had been freed from participation in that and wanted not to return to it. "Others more versed than I were concerned in the matter, Your Highness."

"Many of them have changed their opinion since studying the matter more deeply," he said. I preferred to hear his statement only as explanation and remained quiet. "I would ask of no man that he decide against his conscience, More. Ever have I said that men should look first unto God and, after God, unto me. I will not change. I shall force no man against his conscience."

I could not resist the invitation to study the matter anew when he had so openly declared his respect for the conscience of his councilors. "If you command me, Your Highness, I will study also and inquire what additional considerations have been presented by others."

"Excellent, More! Speak with the others. Study the matter. If your conclusions and conscience permit, I shall include you with those who are now my councilors in this matter." His expression darkened slightly as the words "now my councilors" issued from him. He had not lightly cast the Cardinal aside and forgotten him.

My heart had lightened when he dismissed me. The doubts of him that had grown in my mind were countered by the restatement of his principle that I should look first unto God and, after God, unto him. I applied myself from that moment most willingly and eagerly to the study of his Great Matter. I sought first those scholars known to support the King's views; I heard their reasonings and conclusions and borrowed the books they had written to read in the quiet of my house at Chelsea.

How nearly did I persuade myself? How far was I led by my own eagerness to find all that supported my king and to avoid all that opposed him? By what device was my mind forced back into the past—to the words I had written in *Utopia* and even farther back to the days of my youth in the Charterhouse when I had studied St. Augustine? How did God save me from myself?

I think it happened first that, in the books prepared by His Highness' councilors, I found much of their own opinions but nothing of the opinions of the Church nor the Fathers; and I was reminded of what I had written myself in *Utopia*: "Invariably, kings' councillors are either so learned themselves that they need not consult with others, or are of that sort who think themselves so learned that they will not consult with others." The memory of the words disturbed me.

Then it was that I remembered something of St. Augustine from the dim past. I did not know exactly where to seek that which I remembered so faintly, and I turned the pages of his *City of God*, letting myself glance at each page. And I found first, not what I sought, but something greater, where the saint wrote, "If a man refrain from reproving another who is committing some evil, either because he awaits a more favorable opportunity, or because he fears that he may incite the other to some greater evil, or dishearten others from their efforts to lead a good life, his restraint may be prompted by charity. But he is to be blamed who, though revolted by the wickedness of another and himself living a praiseworthy life, refrains from correcting another either because he fears offending the other or because he will jeopardize his own selfish interests."

The words accused me and enlivened me. Was I not lending myself to the very fault he pointed out? I felt some dismay that I had not entered this study as judge in the manner I should, but merely as loyal servant of the King without regard for the demands of my conscience, so anxious was I to hold my king guiltless. At that point, I put an end to enthusiasm. I was not looking first unto God, as His Highness had directed. Deliberately I reformed my mind. I would be loyal servant to the King, but I would be loyal first to God.

I found that which I sought of St. Augustine: "After the marriage of the first man, created from the slime of the earth, to the wife who was made from his side, multiplication of the human race, commanded by God, required the union of males and females. There were then no humans other than those born of the first man and first woman. Necessarily, then, sons and daughters became husbands and wives, a course forced by natural necessity at that time as certainly as it was later forbidden by command of religion."

Clearly, then, as the holy Doctor attributed a prohibition to the command of religion, he would also hold that religion had the power to dispense. Clearly he established that the commandment, applicable to the King's Great Matter, was not of God as King Henry persuaded himself.

I did not rest with this little but delved more deeply into St. Augustine, then searched into the writings of St. Jerome and other Fathers. Their answers agreed: Holy Mother Church and the Pope had full right to dispense the prohibition against marriage between a man and his brother's widow. The royal marriage was valid.

I had devoted all of my days to the study, for I knew

I was allowed but little time. Yet even in that time did I find more than sufficient reason to offset my eagerness to serve the King. When I was summoned again, a week later, I announced that I had been unable to find cause for changing the opinion I had already expressed.

I was frightened by the expression of His Highness when I announced my difficulty. I dropped to my knees immediately to ask his forgiveness that I was compelled to hold a position contrary to others of his councilors. "Your Highness, I would rather your favor than all of the worldly wealth for which I am indebted to you."

His expression softened, and he motioned for me to rise. "I know none I should rather have joined to my views than you, More. I have said I will not force any man. Neither will I. If you cannot be among my councilors in this, you will yet serve me in other matters as you have in the past."

I had little hope of enjoying his favor in the future despite his forgiveness and his assurance. What value could he find in the counsel of one who had disagreed in the greatest of all matters ever related to him? I returned to the seclusion of my home, hopeful to escape from further involvement.

Again a summons from His Highness forced me from my refuge. I went immediately to York House, which His Highness had claimed of Cardinal Wolsey, and was surprised there to be met and escorted by Lord Norfolk into the presence of His Highness, who waited for us in what was once the Cardinal's study—the room in which I had first agreed to enter the service of the King.

I remember little of what happened this day. His Highness spoke kindly to me, told me the purpose of his summons. I remember kneeling before him and receiving from his own hands the Great Seal. I was made Lord Chancellor of all England.

I was overwhelmed by this new honor, by the King's trust, by the tremendous office itself, and by the show of ceremony that began at the first moment I received the Great Seal. I knew not by what means His Highness had determined on me for that great office except to suspect that the nobles who had gained power together were sufficiently distrustful of each other as not to favor any of their own. The hope rose in my heart that His Highness and all others knew me to be "King's man" without attachment to any other.

Lord Norfolk escorted me from the presence of the King to my place in the Chancery Building. A large crowd had gathered there before us, evidence that others had not been as ignorant as I of the events of the day. They made a great sound as I entered the room, then quieted as I mounted the steps to my place as Lord Chancellor. There, looking down on those faces turned up toward mine, I felt anew the immensity of this new honor and weight of my office.

"I speak for the King," I heard Lord Norfolk say to all those in the room. I could not hold my mind to his words as he spoke. I heard him speak of wisdom, of uprightness and incorruptibility, of wit that had endeared me to the nation and the King. My own mind turned to the stature of this my new office. I remembered how I had stood in awe before Archbishop Morton when he was Lord Chancellor and I a page in his service. I thought longer of him who had immediately preceded me in this office and, when Lord Norfolk finished, my mind was filled with thoughts of Cardinal Wolsey.

"I contemplate this office," I answered, "and think what

great men have occupied it before me. I recall and would recall to you he who occupied it last of all—his prudence, his experience, the splendid fortune and favor he so long enjoyed. I cannot forget his unhappy fall and inglorious end." I related, at some length, the accomplishments of the Cardinal-Lord Chancellor, reminding those present that even one so great as he had proved unequal to this great office and they should expect less of me. While I was yet speaking, I felt the dissatisfaction of Lord Norfolk and ended my speech somewhat abruptly.

"This is neither the place nor the time to praise His Eminence," Lord Norfolk told me when we had left the room. "It is better to remember that he has not yet answered the charges against him."

I dared not speak the thought that came to my mind, that perhaps the King would relent and dismiss the charges, which had come, not from wrongdoing in his high office, but from failure to satisfy the King's personal desires.

"And it is hardly proper, Sir Thomas," he continued, "to praise the man responsible for the King's trouble and England's trouble. To him King Henry is indebted for the scruples that have led him to so much suffering; to him England is indebted that our king must give more attention to the succession than to matters concerning the country."

I did not accept his startling accusations. It is a grave matter for anyone to tamper with the conscience of another. How immeasurable the gravity if a Cardinal undertake it. I had heard the charge before and had attributed it to the Cardinal's enemies. "His Highness stated at the marriage trial that His Eminence had not caused his scruples," I answered.

He laughed without answering, as though he need not

concern himself with more direct answer. His lack of interest was more effective than any other proof he might have
offered. Had he pressed the accusation, I might have been
induced to seek more information. He seemed satisfied
that the future would prove to me what I was unwilling to
believe at the present.

15

I UNDERSTAND now that God suffered me to be ignorant during those tremendous days when I first entered into my great office, that I might better and more readily accomplish His will. To the natural confusion attendant upon my elevation to the highest position in the kingdom was added greater confusion when I attempted to discern the King's purpose in his appointment of me.

Men said that His Highness dismissed the Cardinal because His Eminence had failed to pronounce or to obtain annulment of the royal marriage; yet, the King had appointed me to that same office immediately after I had told him my own convictions. Other men said that I was appointed to hold office only until the King would restore Cardinal Wolsey; but His Eminence was under indictment in the King's own court, charged with violating the King's laws.

My confusion was compounded when Cardinal Wolsey admitted his guilt. I knew his pride that would not permit him in the past to explain his actions. I knew how contemptuous he was of the opinions of others. In this, I thought, his pride could not prevent him; admission of his guilt was much different from mere refusal to explain. Surely, I thought, loyalty and his known affection for the King were not so strong as to make him forget the dignity of his other great office as Prince of the Church. When His Eminence pleaded guilty to the charges against him and appealed to the mercy of the King, I could no longer doubt what Lord Norfolk had told me. I put aside all that I remembered of His Eminence in the past and thought only of the fact that he had acknowledged the charges against him.

When the Parliament opened, thirteen days after my elevation to that highest office of the King, and I received from His Highness the message to be delivered before the assembly of Lords and Commons, I was startled when I discovered it to be a most bitter indictment of the Cardinal.

Deliberately, I put from my mind all memory of gratitude; I thought only of Cardinal Wolsey's plea of guilty and his appeal to the King's mercy. I permitted no sentiment to turn me from the duty I thought to be the King's and mine, to protect the Church and clergy and the Faith itself from the consequences of His Eminence's misdeeds. To the King's message, I added my own bitterness of voice, reading the phrases of denunciation as emphatically as I could.

None could think that the King or I attacked the clergy—again and again, the message repeated a defense of the clergy while it enumerated the faults and failings of the Cardinal.

How easily I deceived myself!

I, who had warned Roper that those who begin against the clergy end by throwing themselves against the entire Church, joined myself heedlessly to an attack against a Prince of that Church. I who had denounced "lawyers' envy" served as voice for a tirade before a Parliament composed of lawyers. I who had been warned about "nobles' envy" seemed to stand forth now in the very forefront of their number.

I read the message well, more effectively than I intended. In Commons, a bill was prepared to cite His Eminence for treason; only desperate efforts by his few remaining friends prevented passage of it. Worse followed. There were prepared in Commons also a series of bills embodying all the envy of the lawyers against the clergy—bills subtly designed for correction of wrongs and abuses, but bills whose end would be destruction of the clergy and of the Church.

Too late I saw the flood released by the message I had read.

In the House of Lords, over which I presided as Lord Chancellor, the members were silent. All knew of the bills which would issue soon from Commons for submission to Lords; all seemed to dread delivery of them. Lay members of Lords seemed uncertain of the role expected of them; clergy members waited efforts of the laity to defend them.

I was reminded that I had been licensed to answer the pamphlets of heretics precisely because a layman's answer is more effective when the clergy are attacked. In the chamber before me, I could see none among the laity willing to expose himself to the scorn and derision of the lawyers in Commons by offering defense of the clergy.

Gladly would I have undone the mischief I had started. Gladly would I have prepared to speak against these bills; but a presiding officer is privileged to speak only at bidding of the King. Gladly would I have assured the clergy members that their suspicion of me was unfounded; as presiding officer, I was privileged to speak only to express views of His Highness. I could only endure the knowledge of my rashness.

When the bills were delivered from Commons and read to the Lords, I delayed deliberately after the reading of each, encouraging some to speak against them. This was the first reading, the occasion when opposition would be most forceful. All were silent. The day drew to an end; the last bill was read; I spoke the formal invitation as to new business preliminary to adjournment, when the aged Bishop of Rochester asked to be heard.

"My Lords! you have heard the bills delivered here from the Common House." His voice was hard as the voice of a man with confidence in the cause he proclaims. "What they sound in some of your ears, I cannot tell. In mine, they sound all to this effect—that our Holy Mother the Church, preserved in most perfect and peaceable freedom by our forefathers, shall now be brought into thraldom like a bond-maid; or even little by little be completely banished and driven out of our country."

The house stirred. I could see some of the lay members moving uncomfortably; others straightened hopefully.

"These lawyers of Commons would have us believe they wish only to reprove the life and doings of the clergy. Why do they not honestly admit their envy of our position and their avarice for the wealth of the Church?"

"Shame! Shame!" a protest interrupted.

The Bishop ignored the cry against him. "I will tell you what I perceive as the end of these bills, my Lords. Unless you resist with your authority this vicious mischief offered by Commons, you shall see yourselves joined to the clergy to be despoiled or shall see yourselves forced to join the despoilers. Then will follow the utter ruin of the Church and the Faith."

Some of the nobles shouted angrily against the Bishop, and others shouted as loudly in support of him. I rapped loudly with the gavel to restore order that the Bishop might continue. But His Grace had finished and resumed his place. I adjourned the session, ending the disorder his words had incited.

The Bishop's speech carried swiftly to Commons. That same evening, a delegation of Commons protested to King Henry that Bishop Fisher had termed them no better than heretics and infidels, and the King summoned the Bishop to explain his meaning before him. There was other work done also that night, for the Bishop had inspired some of the lay lords to defend the clergy and the Church. As soon as Lords convened the following morning, a few lay lords claimed attention to speak against the bills received from Commons.

Others were also at their work of destruction. Later that same morning, while lay lords continued to speak opposition to the bills then before us, I received a message from His Highness: "Appoint a committee of eight—four clergy and four lay—to meet four of Commons and compose differences concerning the bills now pending. The lay members to be appointed from Lords are listed on the attached paper."

I looked at the names he had written. All the hope I had derived from the speeches of the lords defending the clergy fled from me. I waited for the lord then speaking to conclude his speech. My dismay increased with each minute. I, whose reading of the message against the Cardinal had made me seem an enemy to the clergy, was now forced to advance the cause of their enemy. I knew what must follow when the four names His Highness had written were joined to four members of Commons against any four of the clergy. In the four names before me, I saw confirmation of Bishop Fisher's prophecy: "Then will follow utter ruin of the Church and the Faith."

16

FROM that day on which I appointed the committee ordered by the King, I was without friends. The clergy avoided me as their obvious enemy. I avoided those who thought I had joined them against the Church. I was rendered helpless by my office—to express my own thoughts would be to exercise a liberty not permitted the Lord Chancellor. I began each day with renewed dread; I returned each evening to my home downcast. I welcomed the end of that Parliament that had begun actual destruction of the Church.

After that Parliament, King Henry abandoned all pretense of righteousness. At a court banquet, immediately following the end of Parliament, His Highness seated Lady Anne in the place customarily occupied by Queen Catherine. They appeared together whenever public occasions required his presence. The whole country fumed at mounting evidence of His Highness' and Lady Anne's relations to each other. I could believe in him no longer; I could not even retain the hope that he would turn from the life he had entered.

In the year 1530, during which Parliament did not assemble, I had little to do but regret what I had done. To amend for my reading of that message before Parliament, I wrote abjectly to the Cardinal that he might use my letter for his own defense. He answered graciously, but I heard no more of the matter: he was not more interested in defending himself than ever he had been in the past. I performed the duties required of my office and never once had cause to see the King. I walked about the garden of my great house and spent long hours in the chapel I had built. My mind was dull and troubled. Only one action can I claim to my credit—that I refused to join my name to the petition of nobles and clergy to the Pope that His Holiness hear the King's cause sympathetically. It was a most small virtue.

In November of that year, 1530, King Henry began his final assault. Men—"King's men"—were sent north to arrest Cardinal Wolsey for treason. King Henry made clear his attitude by placing in charge the youthful Northumberland, the same whose love for Lady Anne had once enabled the Cardinal to crush the nobles. His Highness dared not only to arrest a Prince of the Church; his fury required also that this Prince be humiliated.

While "King's men" escorted the Cardinal from the north, King Henry struck again by extending the charge of treason against all of the clergy. That tremendous accusation by the King, honored as Defender of the Faith, confounded and frightened the clergy. A few—very few—denounced the King's action publicly; their imprisonment heightened the fear of the others. Some found comfort in whispering that the King was no longer sane; others deceived themselves that he would soon repent of his willfulness and his passion. All comforted themselves that, when the Cardinal arrived in London at last, he would answer ably and dispense the charges.

I allowed my hopes also to rise that His Eminence would defend the Church and clergy even though he refused to defend himself. He had ever been equal to whatever task had confronted him; to him this matter would not be as insoluble as it was to all others. Then came news that the Cardinal would never appear in London. Cardinal Wolsey was dead.

Lawyers and nobles exulted at their victory but, to the people, they praised the King. "Now will you be free," was their song. "Now will you be ruled by a gracious King rather than an oppressive clergy. Now will you be happy with the good things of the world instead of unhappy at those sermons of hell's fire and torment." Well did they persuade. What Luther and his followers had been unable to do in ten years, these others accomplished in ten months. When Parliament reconvened, in the beginning of 1531, the friendless clergy, discredited by lies, had no course but to surrender, to admit to treason despite their innocence, and beg the King's mercy.

King Henry valued his mercy at £100,000. The staggering amount of the fine completed the panic that had seized on the clergy. Without debate, they voted payment.

Unexpected ease of his victory or promptings by his new friends made the King regret his generosity. "You will also," he said in a message to the clergy, "recognize me both as King and as head of the Church in England."

The aged Bishop Fisher—he who had inspired resistance in the House of Lords—and a few more fought to restore courage in the others; but "King's men" appeared to remind of penalties, to tell of the King's anger, and to voice new threats. Panic became a rout. In February of 1531, the assembled clergy voted His Highness head of the Church in England "insofar as the law of Christ permits." Bishop Fisher won a hollow victory in the words he proposed as a "saving clause." The Pope, successor to blessed Peter, head of Christ's own Church, was put aside "insofar as the law of Christ permits."

In my heart, I was also defeated. There recurred to my mind repeatedly the picture of Judas leading a mob to apprehend our blessed Lord—a night when the eleven, confounded by the presence of one of their own as leader of the mob, had fled away. How like to that was what I now witnessed! The Defender of the Faith as the new Judas, the clergy as the eleven. God had been merciful to those who had fled from His side that night; He had brought them back to Himself. I prayed God would be as merciful to these who also fled in the night of tribulation. Most of all, I prayed for God's mercy on myself.

When that Parliament of 1531 ended, I sought Lord Norfolk to beg my release of the King. I was no longer well. I knew not what affliction I suffered. I knew some of its cause but dared not speak of it. I pleaded that my illness would not permit me to continue longer as Lord Chancellor.

I was not released. Sir Thomas More, famed for his virtue, famed as friend of the clergy, famed as loyal son of the Church, could not be permitted to resign; some might conjecture that Sir Thomas More lacked sympathy with the purposes of the King. The name of Sir Thomas More was valuable to the King; Sir Thomas must continue to serve as Lord Chancellor.

17

THE Parliament of 1532 resumed the work of destruction where their predecessors had discontinued. The first business of Commons in that session was to incorporate, in the form of a bill, the Supremacy of King Henry over the Church in England. As representatives of the people, they would imitate Luther and separate the people from their Church and the Pope.

My illness, if illness it may be termed, burdened me. Great ideals towered before me in those days; great fears destroyed them. I was oppressed and saddened to an extent I had never experienced—far surpassing the depression I had suffered in my youth. What I must do as God's servant became more clear and, with it, the price I must pay. I drew back. Had God given me so much only to take it from me? Was God not more merciful? Or, granting that I must suffer, must it be that my wife and my children must also suffer?

Christ had prayed when He beheld the chalice He must drink. I prayed when I beheld the chalice put before me. "Let it pass from me," I implored. Grudgingly, fearfully—without daring even to speak—I resigned myself: "Not my will but Thine be done."

I watched progress of the bill of Supremacy in Commons—the bill that would, by human legislation,

establish King Henry as head of the Church in England
and oppose him to the King of Kings. I prayed the more
fervently, "Let it pass from me." As the bill was read for
the second and the third time in Commons, my prayers
multiplied.

Courage had fled from me. I lay awake nights, in my
great house in Chelsea, in the midst of the family that loved
me, cringing from the visions assailing my imagination.
These were all mine—my house and family—to enjoy
through life or to cast from me.

The bill came from Commons to Lords. The chamber
was deadly silent as the clerk's voice rose and fell in slow
cadence: "Head of the Church in England, insofar as the
law of Christ permits . . ."

Bishop Fisher began the debate. His voice was tired and
weak, much different from what it had been when he had
prophesied so clearly two years before what we now witnessed. He knew the futility of what he was doing—knew
the hopelessness of argument. King Henry had inspired this
bill. The votes of the nobles were sufficient to make it law.

Bishop Clark supplanted the Bishop of Rochester. He
was a younger man, his voice was more vibrant, his arguments more emphatic. What were these against the will
of the King? What force in the realm could withstand that
will? I felt the eminence of my position and the disgrace I
would bring upon it. My fears had paralyzed me; history
would remember Sir Thomas More as that Lord Chancellor
who presided over the death of the Faith in England.

Bishop Gardiner followed Bishop Clark. It mattered
not at all how many spoke nor in what order. The youngest member in the chamber before me knew what must be
done. It was to be expected that these bishops would preach

and thunder; they were the same who had preached and thundered to their fellow bishops. They would be no more successful here than they had been elsewhere.

Only action by the King himself could turn this bill aside. Only were he to send me a message, as he had done before, to speak against this bill, could it be prevented from becoming law. The Lord Chancellor's voice is the voice of the King; the Lord Chancellor's conscience is keeper of the King's. "Look first unto God and, after God, unto me." How well I remembered the words. How quickly had he forgotten them!

My attention returned to the present. The chamber was quiet. Bishop Gardiner had resumed his seat. None others moved to assert their right to speak.

"My Lords!" I knew that I must restrain my voice to that tone with which always I read the King's messages and made known the King's will. The King had used me and my reputation, had furnished that message I had read when I first opened a Parliament as Lord Chancellor, had used me to appoint that committee of lords, had used my reputation to cloak his evil actions. The King had used me and my position for the Devil's ends; might I not this once use my position for God? The oppression within me weighed as heavily as before, but I knew now whence it came. My body and my spirit resisted fearfully while the hand of God urged me forward to His work; between those two crushing forces, my whole being writhed and suffered.

"My Lords! The bill before this chamber has aroused great fears among clergy and people without good purpose." I saw all in the chamber suddenly start as they understood the import of my words. The voice they heard was the voice of the Lord Chancellor, but all knew that the Lord

Chancellor spoke only for the King. "There is no need to identify the spiritual head and the temporal head as this bill attempts to do; nor should we enact into law a bill so feared by the great number of the people."

Some nobles arose from their places and hurried from the chamber. I knew their intent. They would rush to the King or to someone near him and ask his will, unwilling to believe that, so late, King Henry had become again the most gracious prince to his people. I spoke little more. None of the nobles before me were certain what was expected of them; the clergy sat gladly erect. Without apparent care, I pressed the advantage of the confusion among the nobles and accepted motion for a vote before any could think to delay by extending the debate.

The King's voice and the King's will, expressed so often through his Lord Chancellor, triumphed! The one force in the realm that could defeat this bill defeated it!

My mind was clear at last and no longer numbed and dulled as it had been during the night of indecision. I knew what lay before me. I knew also that the courage to contemplate that path and measure it came not of anything in me but was directly of God. He had let me suffer until I would know my own cowardice, my weakness, my fears for my family and myself. Then, as He had intervened with His hand to push me forward to His work, He had provided also the strength and courage to perform it.

My fears were not abated nor in any way lessened. Rather were they increased by the clarity of perception. I returned that day to my great house in Chelsea, trembling and suffering even more than before, comforted only in that I had not resisted God's grace—that I had moved forward as He had directed and had done as He required.

The more painful duty lay before me of telling my family the news they must hear from me before others hurried to them. What should I say? How begin? Remind them of the sufferings of Christ and His saints? Or tell them bluntly that the Lord Chancellor of England had defied his King?

I was spared much of the pain I anticipated. Alice's sharp eyes perceived some change in me before I spoke. I had never thought her talent would serve me as it did then.

"You have won a great victory?" she asked soberly.

I nodded. "Victory to me," I said cautiously.

Disappointment twisted her expression. Tears started in her eyes but she repressed them. "The Supremacy?"

"The Lords defeated it." I told her the events of the day. It was a hard task. We were no longer young. I was fifty-four and Alice seven years older. A misfortune she would have regarded boldly in her youth was made unbearable by her years. As the extent of our ruin became known to her, she could not restrain the tears.

"We will be poor," she sobbed.

The cry was not against poverty. It was the plaint of a soul that had held independence above money and all else. It was the cry of the woman who had said she would rather rule than be ruled, and who saw now that she might be dependent on some others and be ruled by them.

"That will not be for some time, Alice. We have the great house and the lands. We have income from the other lands. If we cannot live as we have, we will still live here to ourselves."

She recovered as her fears dissipated. She raised her head and drew the kerchief from her face. She tried to laugh, and the effort sounded surprisingly like the jeering laugh of younger days. "Did I not once say that I was done with the old manner of my life, Master More—that I would try another manner of life as long as you did?" Her voice resumed the full tone of her old mocking. "Well, Master More, did you think to leave me far behind you?"

I suppose it is God's custom to try us for a time of our own strength—or to let us believe that what we do is of our own strength—until we falter before the tasks and obstacles He sets before us. There He may let us struggle for a time, let us seek help and put our faith in others, suffer injury of body and mind, until we see at last that we are helpless. From those trials we may turn, as do so many, toward some easier way; or hold firm before the obstacle confronting us, sure of His help when our own strength and courage wanes. He had guided me that morning, had stirred my memory to the past words of the King, had strengthened me to do what I must. So, too, had He come to Alice and led her to adopt her old manner of speaking and mocking to enter farther into her "new manner of life."

18

THE fears that had haunted me and despoiled me of sleep for so many nights—fevered imaginings of the King's anger and his revenge for my action—proved groundless. His Highness permitted me to continue as Lord Chancellor through that Parliament; he did not summon me for explanation nor, indeed, for any other reason. Through the office of Lord Norfolk, he sent me the information of the taxes required of that Parliament, and I prepared the bill for presentation to Commons. Not until the session ended did he summon me and command that I bring the Great Seal to him.

He was seated in the garden of York House when I approached with Lord Norfolk. Lady Anne was near him. I was more aware of her anger than of any anger of the King. His Highness showed no evidence of displeasure; rather did he seem disinterested in me and in the incident that had resulted in reclaiming by him of the Great Seal. I knelt before him to speak the formal words asking forgiveness of any manner in which I had failed to fulfill the high office entrusted to me. The words were bitterly humorous.

"Sir Thomas, I discharge and release you of all," he answered. "My Lord of Norfolk informed me that you wish release that you may attend both to the comfort of your body and the good of your soul. Do both, Sir Thomas, and be mindful also of me in your prayers." He spoke rapidly as though to complete an unpleasant duty. He paused for a moment and, when he spoke again, his voice held more expressiveness and warmth. "You were a loyal servant in the past, More. I shall be mindful of that should honor or affliction move you to appeal to me in the future."

He meant sincerely his promise at the time, as he had meant sincerely at another time his admonition that I should look first unto God and, after God, unto him. If I had been guided by my own judgment and my affections, I should have been completely comforted in mind; but I remembered—and remembered without rancor—how lightly he and his father before him remembered their promises. I pitied him, that he who had been born a king had made himself a slave to his own subjects—that he who had been anointed a servant of God had made himself the servant of his own flesh. I pitied him, but without sympathy; for sympathy belongs properly only to those who endure misfortune, not to those who seek to escape their just burden.

God granted me a period of respite after that day of resignation. True, I had now a cross; but, because I felt its weight, I felt also nearer to Christ. At Chelsea, I was able to give my hours to prayer in my chapel, to meditation in the warm sunshine of my garden, to writing, and to the cheering of my family, who could not understand the misfortune that had overwhelmed them, but who were loyal to me who had brought it upon them.

In their eyes, I was not saddened, however much I felt sadness within me. I was relieved of that self-pity which leads us to show others, by downcast expression and slowness of speech and even with tears, how great is our suffering. Of all, I think I was the most cheerful, being the most assured of the providence of God and His mercy. I distracted my family from their fears by planning for them how well we might live for a time and accustom ourselves by the smallest steps to increasing poverty. "We will live for a time on that level I enjoyed at Lincoln's Inn. If we cannot maintain that, we will descend the next year to the fare of New Inn. If that, too, be impractical, we will accustom ourselves to that low fare of Oxford. Then will still remain to us that we go about with bags and wallets, asking alms of good folks who will gladly hear us sing *Salve Regina.*" I said nothing to them of the trial I feared was still before me, and such was the mercy of God that He concealed that trouble deeply within me, where even the sharp eyes of Alice failed to perceive it.

I cared nothing for the world that lay beyond the wall surrounding my great house, for affairs of State, for news of the King and Lady Anne. I was content to remain hidden and secluded except to journey occasionally to visit the fathers at the Charterhouse or to spend some minutes with friends who had fallen ill. Many came to visit me: a few priests to talk of matters related to the welfare of the Church; many friends who refused to believe that I was no longer interested in the matters that had claimed my attention so many years. Some number came to tell me of the new Act of Supremacy, enacted in the year after my resignation. A great multitude hurried to inform me when Archbishop Cranmer annulled the royal marriage; and a greater multitude when the secret marriage of King Henry and Lady Anne was known. I listened but had no difficulty returning my thoughts to God as soon as all had gone.

God prepared me and strengthened me gradually with His grace. He permitted a book to be published by an unknown author, attacking King Henry and Lady Anne and reviling them for their mock marriage. He permitted my enemies to cry out that I had written the book against the King. He permitted my friends to say so also with the thought that the book would seem more important if I were made to be the author. In such manner, God urged me to hurry my preparations.

My mind concerned itself much with the thought of death as was meet for one of my age and, as a first step of my preparations, I wrote my epitaph. "Thomas More," I began, "Londoner born, of common blood but honest stock." I thought back over the past, of the events that had seemed great in my life, of friends, of Jane and Alice. I faltered at memory of my father. So much does the world esteem learning that it little esteems virtue, as though the gate of heaven opened only to those accomplished in literature and science. I could not honestly attribute great learning to him; I could write of him only that he was ever "civil and pleasant, harmless, gentle, pitiful, just, and uncorrupted." I thought long when I had written those words. The one would have been sufficient—that he was just; for that was the word the evangelists had used to describe the parents of the Baptist and the foster father of Christ Himself.

As second step of my preparations, I wrote to Master Cromwell, secretary to His Highness, that I had not nor would I be so bold as to write a book contrary to the King. If I must suffer for good I had done, I could not permit others to attribute things to me which should make me appear a martyr of goodness. Books would not persuade the King against his desires . . . any more than the King's book had persuaded Luther, or my books had persuaded the heretics of England.

God prepared me the more by permitting my name to be entered in a bill accusing me of conspiracy against His Highness. I had greater difficulty countering this accusation than the other, and I saw that God was giving me greater warning so that I would increase the speed of my preparations.

God had prepared me well when the bill of succession was enacted by the Parliament of 1534, designating the descendants of King Henry and Lady Anne as rightful heirs to the throne. When that was done, I knew that more must follow. An act of Parliament alone would not ensure the throne to Lady Anne's descendants; whoever aspired to the throne must have approval not only of Parliament but also of the Pope.

King Henry would know that better than most others and would be more sensitive to the power of the Pope, remembering, as he did, his indebtedness to an earlier pope for his throne. Others—Lady Anne and even some of the Council—might dismiss as unimportant the Pope's influence. King Henry would neither dismiss it nor discount it. He would know that, without papal approval, a future king would sit unsecurely on his throne over a restless nation. He would know also that no pope, present or future, would confirm on that throne a child born of this union with Lady Anne. He would know that a parliamentary bill of succession could establish legal precedence to the throne, but approval of the Church was mandatory to make operative that succession.

Knowing him, I knew the path he would follow. He was not a man who would leave solution of important problems to chance invention at some indefinite time in the future. He was a man who would act in the present to obtain what he desired in the future. He had proved often in the past the force of his will and the power of his determination. Those very qualities that could have made him a saint much greater than our own King Edward or even King Louis of France would drive him to the attainment of whatever goal he sought. He would examine this issue minutely and carefully, would see its weakness, would acknowledge the impossibility of gaining approval of the Pope, would drive forward relentlessly to negate the power that opposed him—the power of the Pope, the power of Almighty God. Until all England and all Englishmen hailed King Henry as supreme head of the Church in England—as Parliament had decreed by the Act of Supremacy—the Act of Succession was meaningless.

My expectations were fulfilled in part when Parliament joined into one the Acts of Succession and of Supremacy, designating Lady Anne's descendants as heirs to the throne and heads of the Church in England. Yet even this was insufficient—Parliament had decreed many laws that had been dishonored by the people.

Through his councilors, King Henry acted to supply the deficiency. A royal decree appeared, requiring all to subscribe by oath to the Acts of Succession and Supremacy. Even this, I assured myself, was not sufficient; the Council had not the power it pretended.

I was among the first to be summoned to subscribe to the oath. I allowed none of my family to accompany me, so sure was I that the Council had exceeded its authority and that I should soon return to my house. I went alone to the palace at Lambeth, beguiling myself by remembering another time I had gone there—a time when I had walked across the bridge with my father, through the open country bordering the river, to become a page to the great man, the Lord Chancellor of England. Now I returned to it with memories of my own days as Lord Chancellor of England. Here had I first told my desire for worldly greatness—that I would be a writer of great books. Here God permitted that I come to renounce all worldly desire.

Some of the lesser clergy were before me—I recognized many among them—but I was ushered before them into that very room where my career had begun, Archbishop Morton's study. Four commissioners of His Highness waited behind a table where once had been His Grace's desk. I felt as though I must quicken my steps from the door to approach the place where I had customarily stood, as I had done in those first days. Then all memory of the past left me. I became alert to what lay before me.

I knew in the first moment that my plan to rest on the Council's lack of authority would accomplish nothing. The attitude of the commissioners voided that fancy. If I challenged the authority of the Council, these commissioners would find statutes by which to charge me with defiance, and I did not doubt that such statutes could be found. A better way suggested itself: accept the Succession, as within the province of Parliament, but reject the Supremacy. I was sent from the room to give the matter longer consideration.

It was a vicious kindness they granted me. To them as to me, my conscience was clear. I could not subscribe to the oath. In the time allowed me from the room, they thought to allow my terrors to accomplish what their words could not. I would have time to contemplate the loss of all my possessions, the poverty that would be inflicted on my family, the discomfort of imprisonment, and loss of that possession dearest to every man, his own personal freedom. I would have time to contemplate that I might avoid all these calamities, for myself and my family, that I might live my remaining years in contentment and even regain favor with the King, if I would but write my name beneath the oath.

Of my own strength, I could not have resisted the offer made me, because my own strength was pitiable against the strength of desire. I depended not on any fancied strength of mine; I borrowed freely of the infinite strength of almighty God. I contemplated all, as the commissioners knew that I would; I contemplated also that our blessed Lord had lived this same trial that I might know the way in my turn. Thrice had the devil tempted Him—with things of the flesh, with vainglory of spirit, with power over the world. Each He had thrust aside. These I must also thrust aside if I was His follower.

My refusal of the oath—which was my refusal in the smallest part and God's in the greater—confounded those men. They consulted and argued, not knowing what disposition to make of the King's former Lord Chancellor. I was sent then into the keeping of a King's man until the King himself considered. Within the week, I was brought to the Tower.

19

G OD journeyed with me. I was strong and purposeful
on the way, gay and mocking to the doltish porter
of the Tower, cheerful when I answered the Constable's
apologies for the poor comfort of my quarters—the man
could not forget my former greatness and some occasions
of kindness to him.

I wrote a letter to my Margaret that I should soon be
released because they who had put me here were not able
to justify their action by law. In the days following, I began
a new work—"A Dialogue of Comfort in Tribulation." So
consoled was I by God that I would share my consolation
with others who suffered. The writing of that sped the
days past, and I was made more cheerful as the number of
finished pages increased.

When I had been imprisoned two months, my
Margaret was permitted to visit me. I was disappointed
when I saw her that she was so distraught; her face had
become thinner and more angular from worry. I realized,
for the first time, that though I was enduring without
complaint because of God's grace in me, my daughter
and perhaps others were suffering in my stead. I exerted
myself, therefore, during that first visit to comfort her
and assure her that the worst that could happen had
already happened.

I think, with that first visit of Margaret, God began quietly to withdraw from me. When I was alone again, I could not resume work on the manuscript of "Comfort." I sat a long time thinking of my wife and my children, of the others who, she told me, had subscribed to the oath, being frightened of what might befall them in view of what the King had done to me who was reputed one of his favorites. Even in this Tower, I was useful to the King!

Margaret returned twice again. At her next visit, I learned of all those great of the country who had subscribed to the oath and was hard put to defend my conscience against her opinion that it was much addled or it would not be at variance with the consciences of others. I would not let her see how much her words disturbed me; but they brought vividly to mind another time when I had agreed that Father Paul must regulate my conscience when my fears had distorted it. Those fears, however, had been much different from my present fears. I feared now mere physical injury and loss of my life, where before I had suffered an exaggerated fear that I would lose my soul. My conscience was now well balanced and in good order.

"Daughter," I answered, "I never intend, God helping me, to give my soul into another man's keeping. Had I studied only lightly this matter of the Supremacy and the oath, I might be excused if I followed the advice and example of others. But I examined all this so long and thoroughly that I cannot let some other be responsible for me."

"Would a humble man so answer?" she demanded.

Memory lifted slightly the sadness from my heart so that I could laugh a little at her. "I will say to you what a great Archbishop once said to your grandfather: 'You are confusing humility with pusillanimity.'"

When she was gone, the sadness was greater in my heart. A man cannot lightly dismiss the actions of others when the others are so numerous. I had to recall deliberately that against their number, I would range the greater number of all Christendom throughout the world; and against the one council of this nation, I could pose all the councils of all Christendom. That effort intensified my sadness, for it seemed that I was condemning my own people and my own nation. God was leaving me more and more to myself.

Margaret's last visit was the most unbearable. She so spoke as to reveal that, no longer my conscience, but now my sanity, was suspect. I think I may have confirmed her fears, because once I laughed when I remembered that those who now doubted my sanity were those who once forgave the King his faults by doubting his sanity.

Those who had first delayed, then granted, her request to visit me had achieved their purpose of plunging me into moroseness that, but for the grace of God, would have sent me into the depths of despair. None believed in me! Not even those who were my own flesh and blood! I had neither strength nor spirit to return to my manuscript of "Comfort." I was denied all human comfort; I felt no longer the comfort of God. I thought that God, too, had abandoned me.

To such depth of despondency did my heart descend that even the light of day, from the window above, mocked me. I closed the shutter, making this cell match the darkness of my spirit. For a week or more, I could distinguish day from night only because of the small light that crept through the spaces between the boards of the shutter. Attendants came in about their duties, and I know they looked wonderingly at me hunched into a small, crushed figure on my bed; but I would not open my eyes to look at them.

After a time, the Constable came, endeavoring to cheer me, but for a long time, I would not answer him nor be comforted by him.

"I will not disturb you again, Sir Thomas," he told me at last. "But darkness is not fitting to a man."

I aroused myself at the word "darkness," which bore with it so many other implications and, especially, that one of which St. John wrote. I forced myself to stir and sit on the edge of my pallet. "When all the stock is sold and the customers gone, what need is there of light in the shop," I demanded.

He did not answer. I sat longer where I was, thinking of that word "darkness" that our blessed Lord and the evangelists had used so often to indicate all that was evil. Slowly and feebly, I revived myself. I was not one who should be in the darkness. I had followed our blessed Lord, and He had promised that those who followed Him walked not in darkness but in the light. This darkness in which I thought to find comfort would only increase my torment. I raised myself at last, forced myself to the window, and pushed open the shutter. The light blinded me, and I thought how like it was to that other light that also blinds even while it directs.

I know now that God permitted me to sink into that blackness of spirit and to draw the darkness about myself. And when I could endure no more, He returned to me. That very day, while I continued in my despondency, though now in the light of day, Alice came to visit.

No sooner did I see her than a last great temptation assailed me. I wanted to cry out—as the Devil prompted—against those who sent first my daughter and now my wife to add to my torments. There seemed no end to their cruelty.

Before the force of that temptation, I could not rise from my pallet, but sat disconsolately.

Alice looked quickly at this mean cell. "I thought you to be a learned man, Master More," she said. "How learned is the man who prefers this to the comfort of his own home? Why will you persist in this?"

Her words were counterfeit. She might deceive others; but I had known her when her tongue was sharp because her spirit was sharp. That was before the day she had told me, "I will try another manner of life." The form of her old sharpness remained in her words, but the substance was gone.

"Would I be closer to God there than here?" I said. The sharpness of my tone matched hers.

My masquerade was more genuine to her than hers had been to me. The tears started in her eyes, and her voice almost failed her. "When will you have done with this gear? I try to follow, but you lead too far."

The Devil had overplayed himself. This woman I could comfort—it were a matter of that small pride still remaining to me that I could comfort her who had never before admitted need of comfort. This woman who was trying "another manner of life" needed God's help to sustain her and, in His mercy, He gave her comfort by giving strength to me! I think, if it be not disrespectful to so think, that Christ sent me in that moment His very own Angel of the Agony to comfort me and lift me up from that agony I was suffering. My sadness fled away; I thought of no more but that this woman who had shared so much of my life and been good mother to my children must be comforted by me.

From that day of her visit to this, I have learned much. From whom? From the One who gave me strength to enter

London in the midst of a plague, who accepted my mute submission in the Church of St. Mary, who pitied the smallness of my strength but greatness of my desire to do His will. From the One who heard my prayer for strength that I would not abandon my responsibilities to pursue my own desire—the One who led me into the service of the King that, henceforth, He might Himself direct all the external circumstances of my life.

I had some part in this—how much I shall know sometime in the future. I had independence to resist instead of submitting as I did. When I put that aside and submitted, I had still independence to accept or reject all that He arranged of the rest of my life; I had independence of attitude toward all that He ordained for me.

I remember that, long ago, I proclaimed the principle that God would direct the life of every man submissive to Him. He has proved it to me.

Do I know all for a sureness? So surely do I know it that I was moved to write as I did to Master Leder: "I shall never be able to change my conscience." I know it from Him who counseled me when I was not aware of His counsel, who strengthened me when I thought I did all by my own strength, who bid me follow Him and gave me the grace both to submit and to follow, who tells me now of my death—I who a short time ago shrank back from that thought.

I know that if I be but submissive, God will accomplish in me the end for which He destined me. I know that, as we imitate our blessed Saviour in life, so will we imitate Him also in death—one to imitate His resignation to the moment chosen by the Father, another to imitate His suffering in those last hours, another to imitate His charity to enemies.

To me it is given to imitate His obedience and to die, loyal servant to the King, but God's first.

I hope all will pray for me, as I will pray for all, that we may be merrily together in heaven.

 **TAN·BOOKS**

TAN Books is the Publisher You Can Trust With Your Faith.

TAN Books was founded in 1967 to preserve the spiritual, intellectual, and liturgical traditions of the Catholic Church. At a critical moment in history TAN kept alive the great classics of the Faith and drew many to the Church. In 2008 TAN was acquired by Saint Benedict Press. Today TAN continues to teach and defend the Faith to a new generation of readers.

TAN publishes more than 600 booklets, Bibles, and books. Popular subject areas include theology and doctrine, prayer and the supernatural, history, biography, and the lives of the saints. TAN's line of educational and homeschooling resources is featured at TANHomeschool.com.

TAN publishes under several imprints, including TAN, Neumann Press, ACS Books, and the Confraternity of the Precious Blood. Sister imprints include Saint Benedict Press, Catholic Courses, and Catholic Scripture Study International.

For more information about TAN,
or to request a free catalog, visit
TANBooks.com

Or call us toll-free at
(800) 437-5876